Sharon Gamble offers readers a valuable resource. This is
to experience. For those of us who are always hoping to discover new and fresh approaches to
delighting in God's presence, this is right up our alley.

— Jennifer Kennedy Dean, author of *Live a Praying Life*

In a world of rush and hustle, Sweet Selah Moments is a breath of fresh air. From new believer
learning to set aside time with the Heavenly Father to those seasoned in the Word, Sharon issues
an invitation to come, savor and learn at the feet of Jesus. Rich with Scripture and laced with
warmth, Sharon's words will help you slow and worship with every page.

— Lee Nienhuis, author of *Brave Mom, Brave Kids*

Looking for rest for your weary soul? The answer lies within *Sweet Selah Moments.*

— J. F. Rogers, author of *Astray*

With tremendous grace, compassion, and gentleness, Sharon encourages deliberate rest and
daily fellowship with Jesus—especially for the busy (be it a bit frazzled) woman. Readers will
take comfort in her genuine transparency and kindness, yet find themselves challenged by her
straight-forward and candid truth-telling. Perhaps the best part? Each devotion is *truly* struc-
tured for the mom with just five minutes to spare before the morning chaos erupts, as well as
for those with quieter mornings who have the opportunity to dig deeper and go further into
Scripture. *Sweet Selah Moments* is sure to have readers reconsidering the importance of rest
as integral to experiencing true joy and connectivity with their King.

—Samantha Arroyo, author of *Fragile: 30 Days of Hope for the Anxious Heart*

Sharon takes you deeper into a more loving, intimate relationship with God. She encourages
you through the Word and guides you in how to experience sweet selah moments. Her
vulnerability is refreshing and impactful. You will love the way she writes—as if you are sitting
across the table from her having tea. Allow the Lord to lovingly speak to your heart through
the heart of this book.

— Fern Nichols, Founder, Moms in Prayer International

This daily devotional is filled with true-life stories and prayers and will be a beautiful
encouragement to any woman. Author Sharon Gamble is passionately committed to
being "Jesus with skin," revealing a God full of grace and truth to her family and to all who
come in contact with her. No one is better at seeing God's redemptive story through the
lens of life's everyday stories, and you will discover practical, helpful insights as you read
Sweet Selah Moments.

— Jere Vincent, President, Family Builders Ministries

Sharon truly lives out what it looks like to "selah" really well. I love her personal stories as
well as her great questions that set us all to pondering how we can do a better job of resting in
Jesus. This book reminds us to take those weekly and monthly "come away" days so that we can
experience the fullness of life that Jesus came to offer us. You will absolutely LOVE this book
and will desire MORE of Jesus, not only by reading about Him but actually experiencing Him.

— Nancy Lindgren, Founder and President, MORE Mentoring

"Be still and know that I am God," is a challenge for all of us living in such a fast-paced, frenetic culture. Yet, once we make the time (yes, we have to be intentional), we are blessed, encouraged, and strengthened. Sharon Gamble is well aware of the challenges we face and provides us with a practical and relevant way of "sitting at the feet of Jesus." Her insights and gentle promptings will inspire and hearten you to go even deeper as you delve into God's Word. Prepare to be uplifted!

— Linda Moore, President and Executive Director, by design ministries

Sharon is full of grace and the ability to give it to you straight. She will tell you what you need to hear and point you directly to the Lord, because she knows firsthand that He is everything each one of us needs. In this wonderful book, she shares parts of her life and much of her wisdom; we all can benefit from what the Lord has taught her!

— Amy Parsons, Editor in Chief, *Strength & Song Magazine*

Sweet Selah Moments is a great tool to help you pause to hear His small voice before being bombarded by the noise of this life. Don't miss out on this wonderful opportunity to daily have a sweet encounter with your God.

— Joel Beers, Pastor of Adults, Eliot Baptist Church

Sharon beautifully describes her desire for every Christian to experience true rest, which is found in Christ. She will engage you with her personal journey of finding peace and rest in the midst of life's demands, struggles, and imperfections. She is gifted in combining God's Word with her storytelling. She can bring you to tears of joy and sorrow all in the same paragraph, as she points you to the Source of our soul's rest. As you read her book may you allow our LORD to draw you ever closer to Him, for in Him is Sweet Selah!

— Sally Burke, President, Moms in Prayer International

In a day and age when our busy lives seem to take priority over everything, *Sweet Selah Moments* is a book that draws us to the value and importance of daily moments with God. As I read through the pages, I found myself not wanting to put it down. I kept saying to myself, "just one more page ...just one more page." Sharon has a sweet, tender and inviting approach that makes you want to sit down and make Selah time a priority. This book will be a treasured gift to anyone who reads it, but especially to those who struggle to sit down and have daily moments with Jesus. I know it has been a treasure to my heart.

— Bonnie Nichols, Founder, Wholehearted

Sweet Selah Moments is an excellent devotional for all levels of spiritual maturity. It is perfect for those who are just beginning their walk with the Lord—the short devotionals are engaging and applicable to daily life, helping the new Christian establish the wonderful habit of starting each day with God. This devotional is also perfect for those who have been walking with the Lord a long time. Sharon's writing has depth, taking well-known spiritual truths and reapplying them with new perspective to refresh our hearts. Sharon's warmth, transparency, and wisdom make this devotional one that I know I'll come back to time and time again.

— Kristi Stoughton, Director of WeConnect, by design ministries

Sweet Selah Moments

ENCOURAGEMENT FOR EVERYDAY LIVING

BY SHARON GAMBLE

Harris House Publishing

Sweet Selah Moments: Encouragement for Everyday Living
Copyright © 2018 by Sharon Gamble

Published by Harris House Publishing
harrishousepublishing.com
Colleyville, Texas
USA

Edited by Jan Peck
Cover and interior pages designed by Kathryn Bailey

ISBN: 978-1-9463-6943-7 (pbk.)

Subject Heading: DEVOTIONAL LITERATURE / WOMEN / CHRISTIAN LIFE

DEDICATION

To my family.
You are loved so dearly.
I count it a high privilege that I get to "do life" with each of you!

. . . .

GRATITUDE

I am so grateful for the support, the encouragement, the advice and wisdom of so many wonderful people who helped me write this book, and who lived through many of the stories told therein.

Lois Wolter, if you had not encouraged me on that long ago day at a conference to pursue the calling I was starting to feel from God to speak and write, I just might not have even written this book.

Jan Peck, my editor and friend and companion, your encouragement and investment in this book has been huge. How thankful I am for late night emails where we hashed out where the commas go and got rid of more overused exclamation points!!! How thankful I am for your deep love of God, His Word, and excellence in writing. Your partnership has meant this book is one I can launch with confidence.

Kathryn Bailey, my daughter and my friend, thank you for designing the cover, the back and the interior of this book while in the midst of adopting your sweet baby girl. Your kindness and giftedness have made this book not only practical, but beautiful. You are beautiful, my daughter, and I love you.

Terry Harris, how grateful I am that you took the time to read the manuscript and pray. I am so glad God told you "yes" to publishing *Sweet Selah Moments*. I can't imagine working with anyone more dedicated, disciplined, professional, and kind. I feel very, very blessed that you chose me to be an author at Harris House Publishing.

Fern Nichols, Nancy Lindgren, Amy Parsons, and Bonnie Nichols, you four have adventured with me and I with you as we tried "new things" these past few years. I have loved having you on the journey with me.

Sweet Selah team and board members, you are indispensable treasures. Each one of you has blessed and encouraged me with your commitment to Sweet Selah Ministries and your hours of volunteered time.

Maureen, Marcia, Lelia, and Kathy, along with many other dear friends, thank you for the encouragement and the faithful, consistent prayers as I've written this book. There's been many a time when one of you was given just the right word of blessing to keep me going.

Bethany, Raymond, and David, I could not ask for finer siblings. Each of you were ahead of me in the book writing department, and each of you gave invaluable advice and encouragement. I love being a Fowler kid!

Mummy and Daddy, I am so very blessed to still have you in my life here on earth. You've encouraged, supported, read and edited, and provided open arms and loving words just when I needed them. I thank God for you!

Mary, beautiful daughter of mine, you have been a wonderful companion and source of wisdom when I needed it as I've worked on this book. Thank you for your prayers and encouragement and your insight as I've written these devotionals. I am so blessed to call you friend as well as daughter.

Ray, your support for me in this new Sweet Selah adventure has been such a gift. You've not only supported this dream of mine by being practically the sole breadwinner in our family, you've prayed. Every. Single. Day. Thank you for wanting to be on my prayer team and then daily *doing* it. I love sitting on the couch, having my quiet time and looking at you, sitting at the table having yours. I love that my husband is bringing me and my work before the Lord, and asking for God's blessing on it. I feel your love and protection as a covering and am forever grateful.

To all of you mentioned and to the many I should have mentioned but did not, *thank you*. May God bless you and reward you for your kindness to me and this little book! To Him alone be the Glory. *Soli Deo Gloria!*

INTRODUCTION

Blessed is the one
who does not walk in step with the wicked
or stand in the way that sinners take
or sit in the company of mockers,
but whose delight is in the law of the LORD,
and who meditates on his law day and night.
That person is like a tree planted by streams of water,
which yields its fruit in season
and whose leaf does not wither—
whatever they do prospers.
—Psalm 1:1-3

. . . .

I'm curious. Do you find it easy to relax? Do you enjoy a bit of quiet and a cup of tea or coffee to start your day? Or are you more likely to race into your morning, trying to catch up with yesterday? Sometimes it's hard to find those quiet moments, isn't it? Whatever your temperament, I'm very glad you've opened this book. It's designed for both the busy days and the lingering days. I'm especially grateful that you're actually reading the introduction because it's truly an integral part of the journey I pray you will take with me through these pages.

My challenge to you is to follow the wisdom of the psalmist and plant yourself by streams of water. Like a tree. Drink deeply from God's Word, the living water. Find a spot each day to meditate on God's challenging, heart-mending, loving, piercing words to you. You will find, over time, that the "planting" of yourself in God's Word will yield fruit in its season. You will not wither. In fact, spiritually, you will prosper.

Whether you are in a crazy busy time in your life or in a quieter season, this book was created with you in mind. Each day, you'll find a way in these pages to meet with God quickly if you're in a rush and a way to linger over His words if you have a bit more time.

Are you wondering exactly what is a "sweet selah moment"? *Selah* is a beautiful Hebrew word found in the Psalms that many believe means to "stop" or "ponder." When you take even a short bit of time to stop and ponder God's Word, you will find one of the sweetest moments of your day.

. . . .

STEP ONE: THE PLANTING

To develop a habit, an action must be repeated over and over again. When we were tiny, our moms had to remind us to brush our teeth. As we grew older, tooth brushing became a fixed habit. Most of us don't have to worry about remembering. We just brush. This devotional guide is designed to help you form the best of all habits: spending time with God every day, even if you only have ten minutes.

If you commit to reading this book through—just one devotional a day—you will have spent 100 days meeting with God. That's pretty amazing. That's the way to develop a habit that will last a lifetime. It's worth repeating—no habit under the sun has more value than establishing a daily time to meet with your Creator and hear from Him. Here are ideas that will help you "plant" yourself each day:

Do it First. Unless you have unusual life circumstances, the best time to meet with God each day is as soon as you get up. Sadly, once your day is launched, it takes on a life of its own. Interruptions happen, plans change, short appointments become long ones, and before you know it the day is done—and all your good intentions to stop "sometime" and sit with God are lost in the craziness of life. If you read before bed, you fall asleep, right? Even if you're sleepy in the morning, let's face it, we do have to wake up in the morning, anyway. What better way to start your day than meeting with God? . . . The God who loves you and already knows the challenges, the stresses—and the joys—that lie ahead of you that day.

Most of us fritter away at least ten minutes every morning hitting that snooze button or checking out social media or lost in thought staring vacantly in the bathroom mirror. We *can* find ten minutes to stop and sit before the world intrudes. You will have time. You'll see.

Make it Cozy. Choose your favorite sitting spot in your home. Have an afghan nearby for soft warmth on cold mornings. Make your favorite morning drink: coffee, tea, ice water with lemon . . . whatever makes your eyes open a little wider so you can focus.

Prepare in Advance. Have a basket or bag tucked by your sitting spot with Bible, pen, and this devotional book inside. Add other books to supplement for the days you can linger. By having materials all ready to go, all the time, you can shuffle your sleepy self to your sitting spot with your wake-up drink. You won't have to figure out where on earth you left your Bible and book the night before. Trust me. It's easier this way.

. . . .

STEP TWO: THE NOURISHING

For the Five-Minutes-Is-All-I-Have Days. These devotions are designed with your varying time schedule in mind. How cool is that? When you know you're facing an extra busy day, open your devotional and read the day's entry. It begins with a passage from God's Word. *Don't skip the Bible verse.* The meat of all I'm trying to convey is found in it, and God's Word is always the "best word," so do read that first. Following the scripture, read the short story or commentary that will help you think about the passage more deeply and apply it more practically. Then, you're invited to pray, asking God to seal His words in your heart. If that's all you have time for, you will have met with Him first and honored Him by hearing *His* words before any others. That is no small thing in a world that screams for your attention. Well done, dear one.

For the Fifteen-Minutes-or-More Days. Hopefully, most days you'll have more than five minutes. On those days, nestle down a little deeper in your comfy spot. Check out the section titled "Going Deeper—for those days when you have more time to ponder." This section guides you into a deeper understanding of the day's topic. You'll be directed to read a section of the Bible that puts the day's verse in a wider context. Dig deep. Read more in God's Word and meditate upon it. The rest of the page contains journaling space to give you an opportunity to become the writer, interacting with the words you have read, processing them, and enriching your time with the Lord.

STEP THREE: THE FLOURISHING

An amazing thing happens when you carefully read, think about, and act on God's words in the Bible. You change. You begin to see life from God's perspective. You realize anew how wonderful it is to be everlastingly loved by the God who is Love. You discover "assignments" God has for you as you sit and ponder. The Word of God prompts you to change behaviors, to mend fences, to speak with courage, to step out of your comfort zone, to reject poor choices. In short, when you read the Bible interactively, responding to what you have read and engaging with it, you will grow. As Psalm 1 states, you will bear fruit in season and prosper. Your leaf will not wither. How cool is that? Who wants a withered leaf? I mean, really. Let's stay fresh and green.

I believe a big part of reading the Bible with the intention of changing and growing closer to God involves writing. Why is that? Why isn't just reading enough? For starters, unless we are extremely well-focused, reading becomes a passive activity. Our brains process the words, but move on so quickly the words don't "stick" in our thoughts. We retain much more of what we read when we write about it. Writing will help you sort through your jumbled thoughts and tidy them by putting them on paper in some semblance of order. Even if it's messy or grammatically incorrect, the very act of writing what you are thinking helps you remember. Makes it more real. Another great advantage is that writing creates a record of your journey with God.

Don't worry about filling the entire "Responding to His Word" section or even answering all three questions of "Going Deeper." Don't worry about whether your words look super tidy or sound super spiritual. Some days, just one question will trigger enough thoughts to fill a whole page. Some days you won't fill it at all. That's okay. Sit and listen. Write as God leads. God's Word is "living and active" (Hebrews 4:12). God will bless you as you seek Him and learn from Him. You will know Him better and love Him more. If you miss a day, don't stress. It happens. Begin again. Even starting over helps reinforce in your mind a desire to make your quiet time an ingrained habit.

I can't wait for you to begin! How about it? Are you ready to spend a few minutes sitting with God for the next 100 days and learning from Him through the study of His Word? There's no time like the present to begin. Go ahead and gather your bag and pop a pen, your Bible, and this book in it. Right now, place

it where you can find it ready and waiting for you tomorrow morning. I'll "meet" you there each morning, unpacking life lessons big and small that God has taught me through some of my very favorite Bible verses. More importantly, God Himself will meet you. Let's journey together, seeking to follow Jesus daily by spending time with Him *first*.

I'd love to pray for you as you start the holy, happy habit of daily time with God.

Heavenly Father, how I love that You see this dear one currently reading these words. You know how many hairs are on her head. You made her. You gave her gifts and a unique and beautiful personality. Please guide her. Help her to hear Your voice. Open her eyes and unstop her ears. Through Your living Word, speak.

Father, we are asking for life lessons straight from You, showing each of us reading this devotional journal how to live in all the fullness You give when we sink our roots deep into the soil of the scriptures. Enable each dear one, Lord, to develop that "holy, happy habit" of daily time with You. For Your glory and honor, I pray in Jesus' Name, Amen.

• • • • • • • • • • • • •

If you'd like to chat about your journey, I'd love to hear how God is speaking to you. Write me anytime at Sharon@SweetSelah.org.

May He meet you in marvelous ways,

Sharon

Day 1

WEAVING TIMES OF REST INTO THE BUSY FABRIC OF LIFE

"In repentance and rest is your salvation, in quietness and trust is your strength, but you would have none of it." —Isaiah 30:15b

Every time I read this verse, memories of my reluctant submission to the concept of "rest" come flooding back to me.

"You would have none of it." That had been the convicting part . . . that was me. Combine a naturally high energy level with a people-pleaser personality, and what you get is a woman who can't say no and who doesn't know when to stop. I gave a passing nod to scriptures that spoke of God's rest, complained of exhaustion with more than a little bit of pride mixed in, and burned my candle at both ends—with a blowtorch.

At about age forty, it all caught up with me, and I ended up in the hospital suffering from extreme and ongoing insomnia. God had my attention. And that's when He began to teach me "selah."

Selah (*See-la*) is a Hebrew word found in ancient songs and poetry, generally thought to be "a musical interlude; to pause and think about [the words] just said or sung; or to pause and watch for a visual demonstration of what was said or sung." (Bible.org)

I've come to believe that taking time to pause and reflect is essential to fruitful living. When I rest in a time of selah . . . life becomes sweet. Since that time of hardship, God has taught me rich lessons about the goodness of His rest:

His greatest commandment is that we love Him. Not that we *do* for Him. When I rest and am still, I have the time to whisper to Him, "I love You," and our relationship grows strong and deep.

Stopping to rest is actually energizing. Truly, "in quietness and trust is your strength." When I shut down and practice quietness, something happens to my body. It is replenished, and I gain new strength. Ready to go again, I accomplish more because I stopped.

Bookending my day with selah time helps my whole day go more smoothly. I start the day by spending quiet time with Jesus, my tea, and my Bible, and end each day with a Christian fiction novel, a warm mug of milk, feet up, and happy.

When I stop for a weekly Sabbath rest, I demonstrate my trust in Him. Will everything really get done if I stop working around sundown Saturday until sundown Sunday? Amazingly . . . yes!

A day set aside for Him replenishes my soul. Once a month I take a "sweet selah day." I might walk by the ocean and admire His handiwork or invest in serious prayer for my family or sing to Him every word of every song on one of my favorite CDs. Oh, how it fills me up and satisfies!

From exhaustion and people pleasing, God brought me to a place of realization that it was more of *Him* I needed. Through rest, repentance, quietness, and trust, I have come to value—and actually love—His command to selah.

You, dear reader, are invited to join me in this journey toward living well by serving with diligence—but also stopping for sweet selah times along the way. All of us need to take time to "ponder the pattern our lives are weaving" (John Baillie in *A Diary of Private Prayer*).

Heavenly Father, sometimes it is so hard to rest. I feel like I always have too much to do. And yet I know You call me to rest. Help me to seek quiet. Protect me from the enemy who would whisper that somehow being still and stopping is wasting time. Help me to see that in being still and knowing You, I find new strength. I want to live differently, Lord. I don't want to be so busy that I miss You. Help me find the quiet spots, Lord, in the midst of busy days. In Jesus' Name, Amen.

· · · · · · · · · ·

GOING DEEPER
For those days when you have more time to ponder

Read Psalm 46.

What calamities are mentioned in this psalm? Is your natural reaction to "be still" during such times? Why or why not?

If God wants us to take moments of stillness even when mountains are falling into seas, how much more must He want us to seek stillness in more "normal" times? What prevents you from taking that quiet time to seek Him and know Him? What changes could you make to be still each day no matter what you're going through?

Pray for help as you seek Him about ways to find quiet spaces in your life.

. . . .

RESPONDING TO HIS WORD

Day 2

FIRST

Very early in the morning, while it was still dark, Jesus got up, left the house and went off to a solitary place, where he prayed. —Mark 1:35

• • • • • • • • • • • • • • • • • •

I don't know about you, but I'm easily distracted. I walk downstairs to start the laundry and notice a dirty glass and saucer in the family room. I put down the laundry basket, pick up said glass and saucer, and take them upstairs to the kitchen, where I wipe the counter while making myself a cup of tea. While the tea is brewing, I remember a card I need to get out to the mailbox before the mailman comes. I grab the card, look for stamps, and then realize I never started the laundry. Or drank my tea. And so it goes . . .

Okay, so I'm not always quite that bad, but . . . almost! Isn't it easy for us to be distracted? Our days are filled with countless tasks and duties—and then fill up with unexpected interruptions. If we don't settle in our minds the priorities for the day, we can fritter it away doing bits and pieces without accomplishing our real priorities at all.

God is quite clear that *He* is to be our priority. "You shall have no other gods before me," He states in Exodus 20:3. Jesus declares, "Love the Lord your God with all your heart and with all your soul and with all your mind and with all your strength" (Mark 12:30). These verses—and many more—make it clear that God is to be . . . first. Jesus modeled this when He prayed very early in the morning.

I'd like to suggest that early in the morning is the best time to meet with God, and here are my top five reasons:

Our best-laid plans are often overturned by the unexpected. We can't always predict (actually, we can rarely predict!) what a day will look like. To be absolutely certain that the first priority—spending time with God—actually happens, let's meet with Him first before the day gets underway.

Our hearts and minds are fresh and uncluttered. Waiting until the end of the day for a quiet time with God often means that our brains are simply too tired to focus. Yes, we can be tired in the morning, too, but morning is the time for waking up, and what better way to do that waking up than with a favorite cup of tea or coffee and the Word of God?

It's a concrete way to show God that He is our priority. By spending time with Him at the very beginning of the day, the very act says, "You are more important than anyone or anything else in my life, so I choose to meet with You first."

My days go better when I don't tumble into them bouncing from one activity to the next, but instead begin with stillness, seeking God's wisdom for my day's true priorities.

I am filled up so I can give to others. When we start the day with our minds fixed on the God who loves us, we start by feeling loved and filled and happy to be His. Emotionally, this prepares us to love those who come our way throughout the day.

Is it hard to get out of bed 15-20 minutes earlier in the morning? Yes, it is. Is it worth it? Yes, it is! The One who loves us best deserves to be . . . first.

Heavenly Father, forgive me when I allow myself to be distracted by lesser things and don't pursue You first. Help me to declare that You are my priority in the way I choose to live my life. I love You, Lord. Help me to love You more and more. Help me to give You first place in my heart and in my life. In Jesus' Mighty Name, Amen.

GOING DEEPER
For those days when you have more time to ponder

Read Mark 1:21-45.

Jesus led a busy life. List every activity mentioned in these verses.

Since Jesus was busy, we can know that busyness itself is not sinful. When does busyness turn into sin?

Are you able to spend time with God *first* each day? If not, how do you arrange your time to meet with Him daily? Write out a prayer, asking for God's guidance about the best time for you to set aside just for Him.

· · · · · · · · · · · · · · · ·

RESPONDING TO HIS WORD

Day 3

JUST LOVE ME

*"The most important [commandment]," answered Jesus, "is this . . .
'Love the Lord your God with all your heart and with all your soul and
with all your mind and with all your strength.'" –Mark 12:29a, 30*

• • • • • • • • • • • • • • •

I've loved God for a very long time. I still remember kneeling and inviting Him to be my Savior at the young age of four. I remember the joy. I remember the finality of the decision. I remember my gladness that I was *His*. Later, at twelve, I walked the aisle and dedicated myself to "full-time Christian service" and chose to be baptized. Even through times of sin and disobedience, I have never wavered in claiming Christ as my Savior.

But . . . somewhere in the midst of living a busy life, that closeness with God was replaced for a season with a sort of "Christian Club" mentality. I spoke the club lingo and was a member in good standing. I even did many acts of service in His Name. But my close relationship with God slipped into mere acquaintance-ship. The busier I became, the greater grew the distance between us. I knew enough about God to sound pretty smart. But intimacy with God? Not there.

I remember clearly the week I attended a conference in California, so excited to be there representing my state. After arriving on a Sunday, by Monday I had the flu so severely that I understood why people die from it. In fact, at the time, I thought that might be preferable to what I was feeling. While all the other women enjoyed great speaking and marvelous times of worship and fellowship, I spent the week in my room . . . alone. They prayed for my healing. I prayed for my healing. I stayed sick.

On Thursday, all the attendees were away, so I shuffled out to the deck over-looking a mountainside. Wrapped in a blanket even though it was warm outside, I was listless and frustrated and sick. Did I mention that part? Feeling like I should,

but hardly motivated to dig deep, I opened my Bible at random. The passage that caught my eye—by God's good plan—was the time Jesus is asked, "What is the greatest commandment?" His answer in a nutshell, "The greatest command is to love God." Yeah. Just. Love. Him.

He whispered to me in that moment, *Do you love Me?* And I whispered back, "Yes, I do." That was all.

I spent the morning doing just that. The most important command. Loving God. Weeping with the joy of it. Affirming that all I had planned to do that week, all the learning I had longed to absorb, all the fellowship I had desired . . . all was nothing compared to the greatest thing.

That time of sickness and helplessness when God asked me to love Him . . . it changed me. Loving Him once again became preeminent. The joy of simply being with Him was overwhelming. Even in sickness.

Every time I am tempted to simply be a part of the "club" again, going through Christian motions without actually noticing God, He reminds me of that day high up in the California mountains. "Do you love Me?"

Yes, Lord, I do! Help me to love You more and more.

Oh, Father, I want to know You more and love You more. Teach me daily. Give my heart and mind the desire to lift You high, to be consumed with You more than any earthly person or thing. I choose You, Lord, to be my dearest love. I love You. In Jesus' Name, Amen.

. . . .

GOING DEEPER
For those days when you have more time to ponder

Read Ephesians 3:14-21.

What is Paul's deepest desire for the Ephesians?

Personalize this prayer by placing your name in the verses like this: "I pray that out of Your glorious riches You will strengthen me, [say your name here], with power through Your Spirit in my inner being, so that You will dwell in my heart through faith" (from Ephesians 3:16-17).

ESV

Now simply sit for a while and tell God the most important thing: you love Him.

. . . .

RESPONDING TO HIS WORD

Day 4

IF I COULD TELL YOU JUST ONE THING

The LORD appeared to us in the past, saying: "I have loved you with an everlasting love; I have drawn you with unfailing kindness." —Jeremiah 31:3

• • • • • • • • • • • • • • • • •

Dear one, if I could tell you just one thing, it would be this . . .

God. Loves. You.

God.

Yes, there is one. Perhaps you already know Him or perhaps you have wondered. Think about this. When looking at a freshly baked cake, no one ever says it "just happened." There was bound to be a baker—who mixed ingredients just so, in a certain order, in specific amounts, and popped it in an oven for a specific number of minutes. In the same way, the more we examine the intricacies of the human eye or the beauty of a sunrise or the precise distance between our planet and the sun that warms us without burning or freezing us to death, the more it makes sense that Someone made this world. Someone made us. We did not "just happen." God made us. God made you. And this God that I firmly believe exists? He loves.

Loves.

Yes. He loves. Why go to all the trouble of creating a world of magnificent diversity and beauty if He had no desire to delight and amaze those He created? Why communicate with us at all?

He loved us so much, in fact, that He actually clothed Himself in a human body and walked among us for a season. Those who witnessed His life on earth believed it with such fervor that, when challenged on their crazy claim that they saw Him killed and then alive again, they chose to die rather than renounce what they had seen. Although tortured, many died singing.

These eyewitnesses were actually eager to declare their conviction that this man had allowed Himself to be killed in their place. They were eager to share His promise of eternal life. All they had to do was simply receive His gift of taking their punishment. And not just one or two, but hundreds in the first century died rather than renounce what they had seen and experienced. Seriously, maybe a few would be that crazy, but hundreds? They actually saw a dead man walking again. He really did return from death with the great news that He had conquered death for humankind and that He wanted His loved ones to live with Him forever. His Name is Jesus. And His loved one is you.

You.

Deeply ingrained in each of us is a sense of unworthiness. A shrinking from the stupid things we've done. A sense of shame over the times we've lied, betrayed, gossiped, and hurt in order to look good or get our own way. We can't even live up to our own expectations for ourselves, let alone others'. We sense that our deeds require punishment, and so we often self punish by reliving our worst moments and cringing. Or we hide by drugging ourselves in various ways, some obvious like alcohol and some subtle like staying too busy to think about it.

Guess what? We do deserve punishment. We aren't worthy. You and I mess up time and time again. I don't know about you, but I'm often super thankful no one can read my mind and see my thoughts. Yet this God, who made us and who deserves our love, chose to take the weight of our disobedience and our yuck as if it were His own. He declared that He would take our punishment. And God did. It's paid in full.

And Jesus lived after dying to proclaim to you that you are loved that much. Ponder one of the most famous Bible verses: "For God so loved the world that he gave his one and only Son, that whoever believes in him should not perish but have eternal life" (John 3:16). You are included in that "whoever." All you need to do is turn to Him and receive what He wants to give: His love, His mercy, His forgiveness, His peace. Fullness of life lived in the understanding that . . . *God. Loves. You.*

I just can't think of anything I'd rather tell you. Ever.

Heavenly Father, thank You for being the living God. I am in awe of Your creation. I am thankful for the witness of those who saw You, Jesus, after Your crucifixion, alive and so well. I choose to believe You are my Savior, and I thank You for the gift of eternal life. Give me courage and kindness, Lord, to share this good news with those I love. Open doors for me and put Your words in my mouth. How I thank You, Lord, for giving me life eternal with You! In Jesus' Mighty, Saving Name, Amen.

GOING DEEPER

For those days when you have more time to ponder

Read 1 Peter 3:15 and Philemon verse 6.

What do you learn about sharing your faith from these two verses?

Make a list of at least three people in your life who need Jesus, the Savior.

Take time to pray for them and ask God to open doors for you to share with them what He has done for you.

Visit SweetSelah.org for a free downloadable copy of this article to give to an unsaved loved one.

RESPONDING TO HIS WORD

Day 5

WHOSE BURDEN IS IT?

"Come to me, all you who are weary and burdened, and I will give you rest. Take my yoke upon you and learn from me, for I am gentle and humble in heart, and you will find rest for your souls. For my yoke is easy and my burden is light." —Matthew 11:28-30

It was while taking a long walk that I finally understood this burden thing. I was definitely weary and burdened. As I walked, I reflected on the hard situations swirling around me. A friend battling cancer. Another friend whose daughter was involved with a dangerous man. My own children were not making wise choices despite all the energy we had invested in teaching them the ways of God. I felt completely defeated. The day around me was sunny and bright, but my heart was heavy.

"Lord," I cried out. "Why is life so hard? Why do I feel heavy and hopeless? Didn't You say Your yoke is easy and Your burden is light?" As I listened for His voice, I heard in my mind, "Because you don't trust Me."

There it was. I had to face the reality that I actually didn't trust Him. The proof was my continued fretting and worrying about how to "fix" all these broken situations, carrying the weight of it all on my own extremely inadequate shoulders. Of course, I prayed, but then I just picked the problems back up and worried about them all over again.

This trust thing is *hard*. When I bring a problem to the Lord and hand it to Him, I need to walk away *without* it. The peace comes when I leave it with Him, contented that He is able to move and change and shape situations as He knows best. Is He or isn't He the only One who can whisper to a human heart? Does He or doesn't He know the beginning from the end? Can He or can't He work horrible things out for ultimate good? Do I trust Him in the messy middle of a situation?

Do I really think I can handle it better than He can?

When I trust Him, my burdens *are* light. I do what I can do: enjoy sunshine on a bright day, send a note of encouragement to my friends, continue to love my Lord, and model what is good in front of my children. But, for what I can't do: cure cancer, restore broken relationships, make people behave . . . I leave that to God.

Father, forgive my lack of trust in You. I am so sorry for the times I come to You in prayer, but then walk away not believing You are able to answer and help me. Forgive me when I don't trust that You are at work. Help me to simply honor You in my daily life, holding on to Your big hand and leaving the running of the universe to You. In Jesus' Mighty, All-Sufficient Name, Amen.

. . . .

GOING DEEPER
For those days when you have more time to ponder

Read Psalm 55:22, Matthew 6:33-34, Luke 11:46, and 1 Peter 5:7-9. Then reread Matthew 11:28-30.

What do you learn about burdens and bearing burdens from each of these passages?

List before the Lord your current burdens.

Ask God to help you let go and trust Him with your burdens. Write your prayer on the following page, using a verse from one of the scriptures above.

. . . .

RESPONDING TO HIS WORD

Day 6

MAKE IT A HABIT

In the morning, O LORD, you hear my voice; in the morning I lay my requests before you and wait in expectation. —Psalm 5:3

· · · · · · · · · · · · · · · · · ·

I absolutely love being a Nana. Since our grandchildren live far away, time with them is especially precious. Often, when our little grandson comes with his parents for a visit, I have the joy of putting him to bed. I love the whole pattern and ritual: Sing "I love you so much" song; say "good night, God bless you" (which he repeats); place his head on little pillow; tuck afghan (made by me!) around him; be sure teddy bear's head is on the pillow beside him; tuck teddy bear's blankie around teddy; give kisses to both. My grandson snuggles right down, because his bedtime routine is familiar to him.

I remember back when my husband was in the Persian Gulf War and my heart was heavy with sorrow and fear. If I had not already established my own morning pattern . . . fix cup of tea . . . curl up on couch with Bible . . . pray . . . I would not have been able to take time with the Lord during those days of huge disruption in our lives. It was so hard to concentrate. My prayers were often pretty pitiful. But, the habit of meeting with the Lord was so ingrained that, at least, I sat there. I read His Word and lifted my heart to Him. And, Oh! The comfort I received was truly a "lifting of my head."

Meeting with the Lord each morning, laying our requests before Him, and waiting in expectation are key to our lives as Christians. Just like you can't drink water one day and then ignore water for the next five days and expect to stay hydrated, you can't meet with the Lord, our Living Water, once a week or so and expect to stay closely in touch with Him.

We need to meet Him daily, establishing a pattern of togetherness, so that each day we receive His insight . . . and His direction . . . and His love . . . and His help . . . for that *one* day.

It's a rhythm that keeps us close and allows us to know God better and better. Then, when crisis strikes, the pattern will be there, and meeting God will comfort and sustain us come what may.

Dear Father, give me the desire and the discipline to meet You morning by morning, waiting in expectation to hear Your voice and sit in Your loving Presence. Help me to lay my requests before You and then wait. Give my heart the stillness it needs to rest in You each day. In Jesus' Name, Amen.

. . . .

GOING DEEPER
For those days when you have more time to ponder

Read Psalm 5.

What do you learn about God's character from this psalm?

The psalmist is struggling with enemies. What "enemies" are you battling? Fear, depression, anxiety, troubled relationships, health challenges?

Choose a verse from Psalm 5 and use it as a springboard for prayer to the One who loves you. What verse from this psalm can you lean on today as you leave this quiet place?

. . . .

RESPONDING TO HIS WORD

Day 7

THE "LOOKS GOOD" TRAP

When the woman saw that the fruit of the tree was good for food and pleasing to the eye, and also desirable for gaining wisdom, she took some and ate it. She also gave some to her husband, who was with her, and he ate it. —Genesis 3:6

At first I actually liked the vine that found its way into our backyard. One spring morning I looked outside, and our wooded area had been transformed into a white bower of flowers and loveliness. I was delighted by this display of beauty. I even took a picture of it, and then, foolishly, I left it alone. By fall, I realized . . . we have a problem here! As beautiful as it was, it had insidiously wrapped itself tightly around tree after tree. Young saplings were weak and some of their branches had no leaves at all thanks to this intrusive vine—which was now everywhere—poking up out of the ground yards away from where it had burrowed in. I was overwhelmed and horrified.

Isn't that just like so many evil temptations around us? No one would willingly walk into a death trap, but how many are lured by promises of "good feelings"? Maybe from alcohol or drugs or sex? At first, the trap "looks good," but later we are overwhelmed and overrun by the very thing that looked so good. Countless people in our culture are snared in traps that will ultimately take over their lives and destroy them. Trust me. It's easier to clip back one vine than it is to eradicate a forest of vines.

This deceptive culture of ours, that promises "good" from evil, is one of many reasons it's important to stay close to the Lord. This is a *battle*. A very real enemy is out there, seeking to ruin lives. Our husbands, our children, our nieces and nephews, our parents, you and I, we all need God's protection and His guidance to see where "vines" are creeping in and taking over.

It's easy to be deceived by a "little" sin. Whether it's prescription drugs or Internet addictions or even gossip or greed, or maybe just snacking that becomes compulsive overeating, each starts out small before it takes over.

One of the best things we can do is to purposefully pray for others—and for ourselves—that we will not be deceived by the "vines" in our lives. Here are some wonderful scriptures to pray:

Guide us. Lord, help us and those we love to trust in You with all our hearts and not lean on our own understanding (from Proverbs 3:5).

Make us aware of the real enemy. Father, may we stay alert and watch out for the enemy of our souls, the devil, who prowls around like a roaring lion looking for someone to devour (from 1 Peter 5:8).

Give us delight in what is good and wholesome. Lord, fill our minds with whatever is true, whatever is noble, whatever is right, whatever is pure, whatever is lovely, whatever is admirable—if anything is excellent or praiseworthy—may we think about these things (from Philippians 4:8).

Bring us back when we stray. Lord, You say in Your Word that You, Yourself, will search for Your sheep and will seek them out. As a shepherd seeks out his flock when he is among his sheep that have been scattered, so seek out our lost children, our distant husbands, our relatives and friends who are far from You. Rescue them from all the places where they have been scattered on a day of clouds and thick darkness. When we stray, rescue us as well (from Ezekiel 34:11-12).

No matter how dark it seems, when we pray, we gain strength and faith to keep going—like Abraham who, *against all hope… in hope believed* (from Romans 4:18). Be a prayer warrior who will not give up, will not quit, will not lose hope, and will continue to pray for loved ones caught in a "looks good" trap. Pray that they will know the living God who loves them and that they will stand firm in faith until Jesus returns.

Now, Oh Lord, to You who are able to do immeasurably more than all we ask or imagine, according to Your power that is at work within us, to You be glory in the church and in Christ Jesus throughout all generations, for ever and ever! Amen (from Ephesians 3:20-21).

GOING DEEPER
For those days when you have more time to ponder

Read Genesis 3.

What progressive steps did Eve take before the final sin of eating the fruit and sharing it with Adam?

Do you have areas in your life that "seem good" but you know are not? What specific steps can you can take, based on what Eve did, or didn't do, to walk away from temptation?

Talk to God and ask Him to keep you far from evil and aware of the enemy who whispers lies to you.

. . . .

RESPONDING TO HIS WORD

Day 8

MY KITCHEN AND ME

I have learned the secret of being content in any and every situation, whether well fed or hungry, whether living in plenty or in want. —Philippians 4:12b

. . . .

When we first moved into our home, now over two decades ago, I found much to like about it. I'd never had a fireplace, and in this little ranch home was a beautiful brick fireplace. My husband liked the wall with a built-in bookcase ready for all his books. However . . . I did not like our kitchen. It was too tiny for a table and had no dishwasher. I caught myself spending way too much time redesigning that kitchen in my mind.

One day, as I was looking around my tiny space, into my head popped a picture of a woman from Haiti staring at me with questioning eyes. I remembered a pastor sharing about his trip to Haiti and that some of the Christians he met lived twenty people to a hut. The hut only had room to sleep ten lying side by side, so those who lived there had to sleep in shifts. They ate and lived outside. Really. Then it dawned on me. My "little kitchen" was probably the size of their hut. The size of their entire house. And the woman in my mind with the bewildered eyes gazed at my kitchen . . . and my three bedrooms and living room and dining room. My complaining heart grew still as I imagined her staring at my home.

My kitchen suddenly looked like a dream come true. We have running water. I can heat water and food on a stove . . . inside, not outside. My refrigerator is stocked with food, and, as a matter of fact, I have so much that sometimes it spoils and has to be thrown away.

My entire perspective shifted with that short vision. *Oh, forgive me, Lord, for my complaining heart. Open my eyes to see how much I have and to be grateful and humbled by it all.*

I can't tell you how many times this visual picture in my mind has helped me in other complaining moments. I focus on what I have—and reject whining thoughts about what I do not have. My heart has grown in gratitude as I notice what God has done and is doing, and I give thanks. You know what? My kitchen is still too small for a table and I still don't have a dishwasher, and I'm okay with that.

Heavenly Father, thank You for every good and perfect gift You have given. Thank You for sunshine and rain, for flowers and birdsong, for warmth on a cold day and enough to eat and drink. Most of all, Lord, thank You that even if all those things were missing, I would still have You and eternity with You. Thank You for the gift of salvation, Lord. Give me a grateful heart and eyes to see all I have. In Jesus' Name, Amen.

. . . .

GOING DEEPER
For those days when you have more time to ponder

Read Psalm 100.

What happens when we "enter His gates with thanksgiving and His courts with praise"? How does that change our attitude?

List some common things you tend to whine and complain about. Then, turn them into a reason for thankfulness. (For example . . . those bills? They represent electricity that fills your home with light or a phone that connects you with your family and friends.)

Look at Psalm 100 again and write a letter of thanks to the Lord based on what He says about Himself in this psalm.

RESPONDING TO HIS WORD

Day 9

LIFE WITH DAD

"You shall stand up before the gray head and honor the face of an old man, and you shall fear your God: I am the LORD." —Leviticus 19:32 ESV

. . . .

The years my husband's father lived with us were a tremendous blessing. In his 90s, Dad was sound in mind, but his dear body was failing. Unable to stand or walk, he needed help with most daily tasks. God used this season of caregiving to teach me abundant lessons, and I will be forever grateful that Dad joined our little family here in New Hampshire. In my time with him, I learned . . .

Be kind. Dad was a kind person. Whether it was a visiting nurse, an aide, or one of us caring for him, he was quick to say thank you and slow to complain. Guess what? People *liked* to take care of him because of his attitude. If I'm ever the one who needs full care, I hope and pray that I will be kind and pleasant like he was. So, I'm practicing up on kindness now.

Life is short. Savor each day. At that stage in his life, Dad never took his days for granted. He treated each one as the treasure it was. Whether savoring that first cup of coffee in the morning or watching leaves turn green, then gold in the autumn, Dad noticed and commented. Because of him, I, too, began noticing and commenting.

Slow down. Before Dad moved in, I hurriedly ate my breakfast and lunch. Even dinner was a quick affair, done in 20 minutes or less. This was not the case with Dad. He found it difficult to eat quickly. A typical lunch or dinner would take at least an hour. When he first moved in, I had a choice. Would I eat until I was done and leave him to eat alone? Or would I slow down and give him the courtesy of company? We did have breakfast separately, but lunch and dinner were . . . long. After a few months of squirming on the inside at this snail's pace, I settled into a new habit of eating slowly, digesting, and commenting on life. I still like it that way.

Plan ahead. With Dad, "just going out" was a complete impossibility. First, I needed to change his oxygen to the portable tank, then affix the footrest to his wheelchair, gather various pieces of paraphernalia, and transport him into the wheelchair van. This meant my days required planning ahead and not just diving in willy-nilly. It turns out that having a plan is actually less stressful than the chaos that often ensues with last-minute decisions.

It's not about me. Of course, in theory, I've known this since I was about two years old whether I liked it or not. In practice, I'll admit, I've had times when I've been able to arrange life to suit myself pretty well. Life with Dad did not fall into that category. Having to think about how another human being feels, having to anticipate his needs, having to put his comfort ahead of my own turned out to be actually quite valuable. Caring for others brings more joy than a self-focused lifestyle ever could. We tend to grow too fussy when we have only ourselves to worry about and pamper.

Say yes to help. My husband, Ray, and I didn't often ask for help, but when it was offered in the form of a meal or a time away, we said yes. We were also blessed to have aides who helped in the mornings. How easily we might have thought that we were the only ones who could care for him—and wear ourselves out in the process. We learned that we are not indispensable, and we cannot do it all alone.

God sustains. The very nature of caregiving is tiring. Whether you are caring for a child or an aging parent, the constancy of the care can grow wearisome. How deeply we need to seek God and rely on *His* strength! Daily quiet times, reading His Word, remembering how constantly He cares for us . . . those things sustain us. Taking days off from caregiving, listening to God's voice through song and book and quiet . . . these things restore us. We cannot do this with glad hearts without allowing the love of God to be poured into us and then out again through us. God helped us and held us, and we were blessed to have Dad in our home.

Heavenly Father, You are the source of love, joy, peace, patience, kindness, goodness, faithfulness, gentleness, and self-control. These don't always come naturally. Fill me with the fruit of Your Spirit, Lord, that I might pour it out on those I love. Forgive me when I choose self-centered, angry responses to those under my care. Help me to love like You love.

Show me when to rest and when to work. Sustain and help me, Lord, day by day. I need You every minute. In Jesus' Name, Amen.

- - - - - - - - - - - - - - -

GOING DEEPER

For those days when you have more time to ponder

Read Galatians 5:16-26.

Slowly read through verses 19-21. If any of these apply to you, confess and be forgiven.

Review the fruit of the Spirit listed in verses 22-23. Ask God to grow every one of these qualities in your life.

Focus on the fact that, if you are a Christian, God's Spirit is within you, with you, each moment of every day. Ask God to help you remember His presence all day long, and speak to Him often, just as you would to a friend beside you. Keep in step with His Spirit today, as you serve others who cross your path.

- - - - - - - - - - - - - - -

RESPONDING TO HIS WORD

Day 10

THAT TIME I WAS KIDNAPPED

*Carry each other's burdens, and in this way you
will fulfill the law of Christ. —Galatians 6:2*

. . . .

Life was not going well with me. At all. My college child was hurting and that meant I was hurting. I tried to help, but often made things worse, smothering her at times with my suggestions and well-meaning advice. I felt defeated. I felt like a huge failure as a parent. And my Moms in Prayer* group noticed my heavy heart.

So, one Saturday morning, I got the kidnapping call. "Be ready in an hour, Sharon. We're coming to your house, picking you up, and driving you to Prescott Park for some serious prayer time . . . for you." My group leader at the time sounded so serious that I didn't even raise a protest, though the last thing I wanted was a trip to the park when I was feeling so dispirited about life. I can't remember for sure, but I think at least two cars were involved. A lot of women came to my kidnapping.

Off we went to beautiful Prescott Park in New Hampshire. First, we simply walked and talked, admiring the fall flowers and enjoying each other's company. I was still in shock that so many women had given up a Saturday morning to devote to my well being. Even today, I grow teary-eyed remembering their gift of time. We stopped at a bench, and, with women surrounding me, the interceding in one accord began. Those dear friends prayed their hearts out for me. They prayed in agreement, all lifting me up to the Prince of Peace, Lord of lords, who alone could carry my heavy burden. I was pretty teary-eyed then, too.

You see, I felt beaten down. I couldn't seem to get up. My friends cried out on my behalf, lifting my troubles to the Lord, who lightened my load through their faith-filled prayers. They took me home a changed woman. How thankful I am for that day! Truly a turning point for me. I was empowered to keep on praying for my girl. Best kidnapping ever.

Sometimes our burdens seem too heavy to carry alone. Guess what? God has placed us in His family for a reason. As Christians, we have other sisters we can call upon to help us pray when life just seems too much. Do you have women you can turn to in a crisis who will pray with you? If not, I encourage you to seek out a Moms in Prayer group near you or a Bible study group where prayer is an integral part. We need each other. Let's carry each other's burdens, shall we?

Pray with me.

Father, forgive me when I feel too busy to stop and help a hurting sister in Christ. Show me the women for whom you wish me to pray. And Lord, forgive me too, when I foolishly try to struggle alone instead of reaching out and asking for help along the way. Thank You for Christian family. Show me the women in my area You would choose for me to know in this deeper way of prayerful living. In Jesus' Name, Amen.

GOING DEEPER
For those days when you have more time to ponder

Read Mark 2:1-12.

What do you learn about the friends of the paralytic man and their determination to help him?

How did Jesus respond to this man, who was brought by his friends?

Is there anyone you know who might benefit from a kidnapping like mine? Ask the Lord if this might be something He would have you do. If it is, do it!

*Moms in Prayer International is an organization that brings mothers and grandmothers together once a week to pray for the lives of their children, their grandchildren, and their teachers and schools. For more information, visit MomsInPrayer.org.

RESPONDING TO HIS WORD

Day 11

GOOD PLANS

*Do not those who plot evil go astray? But those who plan
what is good find love and faithfulness. —Proverbs 14:22*

. . . .

I am finally going to lunch with a friend after almost a year of saying, "We just have to get together." I cannot believe how long it has taken. The reason? Pretty simple. We didn't plan it. We just talked about it. Once we looked at our calendars and set a date, it happened.

I must plan to do what is good.

Many years ago when my husband, Ray, retired from the military and we finally lived near our families again, I realized I was not making time to visit our parents. I meant to, of course, but with two busy girls and all their activities, it was easy to simply postpone visits with parents . . . sometimes weeks on end. One day, I stopped to weigh this busyness against the importance of honoring parents, and I was ashamed of the choices I had made.

That's how Wednesdays became "Parent Day." Fortunately, both our parents lived only a mile from each other, so we visited my dear folks first and then Ray's. For many years, we all looked forward with great delight to those Wednesday visits and what sweet memories we made. I still regularly visit my parents, and, during the time Ray's dad lived with us, he could always count on Wednesdays for something fun. When it's on the calendar, it happens.

Good things happen when I plan.

What about time with God? Does that just happen? Nope. Spending time with God, my number one priority, requires planning. Here are some reminders and suggestions that will help you plan to do the "best good" of all, which is to spend time with the God who loves you and who tells you that His greatest commandment is to love Him with all your heart and soul and mind:

Pick a daily spot where you will meet with God, and put your Bible and journals and devotion book and a pen right there in a bag or in a drawer nearby ready for use. Plan this out so it will happen.

Arrange your time. Whether it's a 10-minute or a 50-minute time slot, set your alarm accordingly. If mornings won't work for some reason, make a plan for the same time each day that you will spend with Him.

Expect this to be a pleasant time. I love cups o' tea, so part of my plan is to brew a cup of tea and sit in my most comfortable chair (the one where I can put my feet up) while I meet with my God and King.

Stay consistent. On vacation or visiting someone? Keep to your plan anyway. I always scout out the best Quiet Time spot the night before, making sure my little bag of Quiet Time books and my Bible are ready for me there.

We can so easily let one day drift into the next, busy with the urgent tasks—and the mundane tasks—that make up our lives. Then, one day we look back and realize we did not make time for what mattered most of all. It won't just happen. Make a plan. You'll be glad you did.

Heavenly Father, forgive us when we only pay lip service to what is most important. Help us to actually do the most important. Give us a plan that works within the framework of busy days and schedules. Oh, Lord, create in us a longing to sit at Your feet and learn from You—the One who loves us so dearly. In Jesus' Name, Amen.

. . . .

GOING DEEPER
For those days when you have more time to ponder

Read Mark 6.

List some of the reasons Jesus might have said to His disciples, "Come with me by yourselves to a quiet place and get some rest" (v. 31).

What happened when they tried to get away and how did Jesus respond to the unexpected?

Reread verses 45-46. What does Jesus' example tell us about making a plan to rest? What's *your* plan—and your backup plan?

· · · · · · · · · · · · · · ·

RESPONDING TO HIS WORD

Day 12

YOU ARE LOVED

And I pray that you, being rooted and established in love, may have power, together with all the Lord's holy people, to grasp how wide and long and high and deep is the love of Christ, and to know this love that surpasses knowledge. —Ephesians 3:17b–19a

• • • • • • • • • • • • • • • •

It's not always easy to show love to others. Some days it's downright hard. For me, it's tough to show love when:

Illness has worn me down, and I feel too sick to react with kindness.

My sleep has been continually interrupted. I can remember waking to a screaming baby and begging God for patience and kindness when all I wanted was to block out the noise, sleep . . . and ignore my poor baby's needs. (I did get up, but it wasn't easy.)

My expectations aren't met. When my heart is set on something, and I assume my husband or child will agree, but they don't . . . feeling anger toward them comes more naturally than love.

Someone is unkind to me—intentionally or unintentionally. My first thought is to strike back.

Basically, it would seem, I'm best at loving when I feel loved. Otherwise, I'm pretty terrible at it. But God has taught me one of the most valuable lessons of my life: The only way I am able to give love is to first sit at His feet and receive His love.

Each morning, when I settle onto my couch, cup of tea in hand, and Bible open, I am reminded that I am deeply loved. Flaws and all. This truth seeps into me as I read Bible stories of people like David, who failed and failed, but were forgiven and loved. I know God's love when I read of Jesus' life and sacrifice for me. Passage after passage reminds me that God. Loves. Me. And I don't even have to be "worthy." I'm not. But the Shepherd of my soul tenderly cares for me anyway.

Dear one, you are loved. Your God loves you so deeply that He left Heaven, put on a human body, and died for you, so that you could live with Him forever. Over and over in the Bible, He declares His love for you. It is higher, deeper, longer, and wider than anything we can even fathom. His love does not depend on your efforts or your worthiness. He made you and knows you and, while you were still a sinner, before you even attempted anything good, He died for you. Believe it.

In his letter to the Ephesians, Paul prays that we may be rooted and established in love. Roots secure the plant, so that it doesn't blow away. Roots draw up nourishment from the earth. When we are rooted and established in love, we aren't easily blown away. We are nourished by God's love, and then we are able to give out that love to others.

Today, whether you feel loved by fellow humans or not, remember that you have a Father who loves you. He loves you because you are His child. He loves you regardless of your accomplishments or failures. "But when the kindness and love of God our Savior appeared, he saved us, not because of righteous things we had done, but because of his mercy" (Titus 3:4-5a). You. Are. Loved.

Thank You, Father, for a love beyond our comprehension! Help us to rest in that love, sure in the knowledge that You do not change Your mind like we do. Your love is forever. In the Name of Jesus, who showed that love sacrificially, we thank You. Amen.

* * * * * * * * * * * * * * * * *

GOING DEEPER
For those days when you have more time to ponder

Read 1 Corinthians 13.

Write down the times it's hardest for you to love. Ask for God's help to make changes.

Thank Him for His love for you by praying the verses in 1 Corinthians 13:4-8a: Lord, thank You that You are patient and kind with me. You don't envy. You don't boast. You have every reason to be proud, but instead You humbled Yourself and became a little baby here on earth. You are not rude. Instead of self-seeking,

You sought lost ones like me. You are not easily angered. You don't keep a record of sins. You forgive them. You paid for them Yourself on the cross. You do not delight in evil. You are the just Judge of the earth. You rejoice when we embrace Truth. You always protect, are always trustworthy, always inspire hope, and Your love always perseveres. Your love never fails.

How are you doing at believing that God loves you? Ask Him to impress that truth upon your heart so that, out of a deep assurance that you are loved, you are set free to love others through Him.

. . . .

RESPONDING TO HIS WORD

Day 13

ONCE UPON A TIME

For the word of God is alive and active. Sharper than any double-edged sword, it penetrates even to dividing soul and spirit, joints and marrow; it judges the thoughts and attitudes of the heart. —Hebrews 4:12

• • • • • • • • • • • • • • •

Once upon a time, there were two boys named Sam and Tom. Each one lived in an age when dragons roamed, princesses needed rescuing, and swords were necessary for heroic deeds. Each boy had been left a sword by his father.

Sam picked up his dad's sword and found it heavy and awkward. It hurt his hand and his wrist. "This sword doesn't work," he declared. So, he decided to become a farmer and leave swords to someone else.

Tom picked up his dad's sword and found it heavy and awkward. It hurt his hand and his wrist. "My hands aren't strong enough to handle this sword," said Tom. So, he practiced with the sword every day, strengthened his hands, and learned how to wield the sword with great skill.

One day, a dragon came into their valley. Sam hid from the dragon while it destroyed his farm. Tom went out and fought the dragon with his sword and saved himself, his family, and his village. Then, Sam asked Tom to help him learn to handle the sword. He practiced diligently, determined to be ready the next time the dragon attacked. And, as in all good stories, they all lived happily ever after, grateful for a weapon against the enemy.

Hebrews 4:12 declares that the Bible is alive and active, sharper than any two-edged sword. We've been given a very real weapon to wield against a very real enemy, the enemy of our souls, referred to in the Bible as a dragon, even! "The great dragon was hurled down—that ancient serpent called the devil, or Satan, who leads the whole world astray" (Revelation 12:9a).

Like Sam in our story, we often find reading God's Word tiresome and "heavy" when we first begin. We have no idea how to utilize scripture against the schemes of the devil. So, we wander away and leave ourselves vulnerable to attack.

Our Lord Jesus brandished scripture during His time of temptation in the wilderness. He knew God's Word through and through, and He declared truth to the tempter. Following His example, let's study His Word so that, when the enemy whispers lies, we are ready to wield "the sword of the Spirit, which is the word of God" (Ephesians 6:17b).

Here are two examples of enemy tactics:

The attack: "You're not worthy of love. You're pathetic. God can't forgive you."

The Sword: "But God demonstrates his own love for us in this: While we were still sinners, Christ died for us" (Romans 5:8).

The attack: "You've prayed and prayed and nothing happened. Give up. God doesn't hear."

The Sword: "Then Jesus told his disciples a parable to show them that they should always pray and not give up" (Luke 18:1).

Heavenly Father, help me learn how to wield the Sword. Show me the scriptures I need to fight the enemy of my soul. Remind me, Lord, in the midst of an attack, so that I can fight back using Your Word. Strengthen my weak hands, and use me as a warrior on my knees for Your Kingdom work. In the mighty Name of Jesus, Amen.

. . . .

GOING DEEPER
For those days when you have more time to ponder

Read Matthew 4:1-11.

List the three temptations that Jesus faced. How are they similar to temptations you face?

List areas in which you see yourself as vulnerable to attack, such as unbelief, anger, or worry. Then, ask the Lord to show you a scripture or two that you can use against the enemy whenever the thought pattern appears that causes you to sin.

Take time to pray; ask God to remind you of His Word when you feel attacked; ask Him to reveal more and more scriptures you can cling to in hard times.

· · · · · · · · · · · · · · · · ·

RESPONDING TO HIS WORD

Day 14

HOW GOD TREATS ANXIOUS PEOPLE

When anxiety was great within me, your consolation
brought joy to my soul. —Psalm 94:19

. . . .

Dear Anxious One,

Do you beat yourself up—and even grow anxious about your anxiety? Do you read verses like Philippians 4:6, "Do not be anxious about anything" and feel like a total failure? Do you find it hard to explain to people that you don't look for anxiety . . . it looks for you and grips you and shakes you like a pit bull, not letting go? Just let your eyes read Psalm 94:19 slowly . . . with wonder.

When anxiety was great within me,
your consolation brought joy to my soul.

This, dear friend, does not sound like a God who is angry with the anxious guy who wrote Psalm 94. Let's take a closer look together.

When anxiety was great within me. The psalmist talks about his anxiety matter-of-factly. Openly. He even admits that his anxiety isn't trivial—but a great, big, huge thing stuck inside him. His anxiety is all-consuming, and he seems to have no shame in sharing this. It's a fact. He had great anxiety. Everyone has troubles of one sort or another. Some of us struggle with a quick temper. Some of us have to work through melancholy. Others want to talk on and on, when perhaps we should listen more (ahem). Our temperaments predispose us to certain maladies. People who feel deeply, which is not a bad trait at all, often fight anxiety—which is a hard thing, a suffering thing. Sometimes, I think we make our troubles worse when we don't admit we have them.

Your consolation brought joy to my soul. Do you hear these sweet words from the God who loves you? In the very midst of his anxiety, while still in its grip, God consoled him. Right there. Right then. While it was still "great" within him.

That consolation was a solace that brought joy to his soul. The hidden message is that the psalmist didn't run from God in shame and fear and self-loathing. He acknowledged his anxiety, turned toward God, and received consolation.

Too often, your enemy the devil compounds the offense of anxiety with the burden of shame. And you lose twice. Anxiety *and* Blame. Of course, God doesn't want us to be anxious. Scripture is full of His instructions on ways to overcome it, and almost every time, He calls us to bring our cares to Him. Still, at times, anxiety intrudes.

Savor the words in this beautiful psalm, dear anxious one. How does God treat anxious people? He consoles them. Let that fill your heart with joy.

Dear Father God, thank You for consoling anxious people. Thank You for bringing joy right in the midst of scary times. Thank You that Your answer is always, "Come to Me." Thank You for a deep, lasting, kind love that enfolds and comforts and teaches and helps. Help those reading this today who struggle with anxiety. May they sense Your consoling love. In the name of the Good Shepherd, Jesus, Amen.

. . . .

GOING DEEPER
For those days when you have more time to ponder

Read Psalm 94.

The psalmist begins with cries of great depression. At what verse does he switch gears and begin trusting God?

How does he remind himself to trust in anxiety-laden times?

Are you prone to anxiety? Or, do you know someone who is? Stop and pray, asking for God's consolation and help to grow in trust.

RESPONDING TO HIS WORD

Day 15

WILL YOU HOLD MY HAND?

For I am the LORD your God who takes hold of your right hand and says to you, Do not fear; I will help you. —Isaiah 41:13

. . . .

He's seen too much in his short, little life. Lived in too many homes; had too many families to ever feel secure. For a season, he lived with my daughter and her husband and their son. They often open their home to foster children who have no other place to go.

Finally, one summer, I met him for the first time. We don't live near each other, so phone calls and pictures fly back and forth, but actual visits are treasured and rare, carefully planned and anticipated. Oh, how I wanted our visit to go well! How would he respond to the new, temporary grandmother figure in his life? Would he call me Nina like my other grandchildren do? Would he sense my love and joy in meeting him? Would he . . . let me hug him?

Yes. He did. We hugged, we laughed together. He let me hold him. And every time we crossed the street to the beach, he said, "I want to hold Nina's hand." I felt a ridiculous amount of joy with that little boy's hand in mine. How I'd longed to be with him and get to know him and show him how dearly he is loved. Our time together is one of those sweet memories that stays in my mind. One day, in my very old age with time on my hands to remember, I shall pull it out and dust it off. I'll remember the feel of sticky little boy hands clinging tightly to mine as we crossed a busy road.

Sometimes I feel worn down by all the hard and horrible things happening around me—happening to ones I love. The world can be a scary place, and the amount of pain in people's lives can be overwhelming.

Maybe you find yourself in a hard, scary, or painful place today. Maybe you are the one with a sticky hand and a worried heart. Let's be the little ones who look up at our Father and say, "Will You hold my hand? Please don't let go."

We don't walk alone. We have our Abba Father with us, whispering, *"Do not fear; I will help you."* With our hand in His, we can cross any street of difficulty.

One day, I hope this little boy finds a permanent place of belonging. Some sweet day, I hope he learns to trust his Heavenly Father and slips his little hand into the hand of the One who will truly be his Helper—the One who will be with him always and love him most of all. I hope you and I keep our hands in His as well.

Dear Heavenly Father, thank You for being the kind of Father who holds His children's hands and who whispers, "Do not fear; I will help you." You are good. You are strong. And You allow us to call You Abba Father. Thank You for loving us so tenderly. Help us remember that You hold our hands. In Jesus' Name, Amen.

GOING DEEPER
For those days when you have more time to ponder

Read Isaiah 41:1-16.

In these verses, the Lord declares Himself to be "in charge." Write down the key phrases that remind you He is totally in control.

In the passage, God begins by proclaiming who He is and how powerful He is. Then He begins to comfort His people. What does God reveal about the way He will take care of His own?

Write a prayer thanking Him for His help and His hand in troubled times.

RESPONDING TO HIS WORD

Day 16

FIERCE LOVE

Can plunder be taken from warriors, or captives be rescued from the fierce? But this is what the LORD says: "Yes, captives will be taken from warriors, and plunder retrieved from the fierce; I will contend with those who contend with you, and your children I will save." —Isaiah 49:24-25

• • • • • • • • • • • • • • • • • •

Before I had children, I didn't understand how fierce a mother's love could be. I loved my Ray—and oh, I still do! I thought I had a good understanding of love . . . and then I had my first baby. I suddenly realized how different a parent's love is.

I had never thought of myself as a forceful woman. I try to be nice. I like being kind. But at the thought of someone harming one of my babies, a fierce protectiveness awoke in me. I knew if someone tried to injure my child, I would defend her at the cost of my own life. No one would hurt my little one as long as I had the power to stop it. A unique, fierce kind of love arose from the neediness of my helpless infant, and that love was different from my love for her daddy.

When God calls Himself Father, He shows how full and rich His love for us is. God calls us His children. Do you see what this means? His is a parent's love; His love for us is *fierce*. We are His needy and helpless children, and this verse in Isaiah assures me that our God will contend for us and save us—and our children.

To *contend* means to "fight with," "struggle against," or "deal with." I tremble for those who mess with God's children. Jesus Himself said that it would be better for them to have a large millstone hung around their neck and to be drowned in the depths of the sea, than to cause a child of His to stumble. You, dear one, are His child if you have accepted Him as Lord and Savior. Let's pray for those among us who are cruel and abusive and those who lead our children astray.

Their punishment will be severe if they do not repent, for God's love is that fierce.

As you go about your day, remember that you have a loving Father who is protective of you and who will contend with those who contend with you. Wow. May the fierceness of His Father-love comfort you.

Heavenly Father, I stand amazed that You care so deeply for me. Thank You for a fierce, protective love that will endure forever. Thank You that it does not depend on my merit, but on Your mercy and forgiveness. Oh, Lord, turn the hearts of those who are cruel to Your children. Help them repent while there is still time. In Jesus' Mighty Name, Amen.

GOING DEEPER
For those days when you have more time to ponder

Read Matthew 18:1–14.

Ponder what it means to come to Jesus as a child. What personal qualities would it take for that to be a reality in your life?

Why is Jesus so fierce in His warnings? What does that say about future judgment for those who do not repent?

What do you learn about God's love for each individual from the story of one lost sheep in a fold of one hundred? As you reflect on this passage, write God a prayer; fill it with gratitude, as well as with any questions you might have for Him.

RESPONDING TO HIS WORD

Day 17

DAILY CHOICES

"Choose for yourselves this day whom you will serve, whether the gods your ancestors served . . . or the gods of the Amorites, in whose land you are living. But as for me and my household, we will serve the LORD." —Joshua 24:15b

• • • • • • • • • • • • • • •

It was my own daughter who taught me a life lesson about the big difference "small" choices can make. Some years ago, I was leading a prayer group for high school girls—and we had a guest speaker: my daughter Mary, who was home visiting from college.

Mary talked about how little, daily choices made in college can have big, and sometimes unintended, consequences. She gave the example of the choice to stay up late every Saturday night. This, in turn, makes it hard to attend church or to enjoy church if you drag yourself there on a Sunday. This, in turn, influences many college students to simply stop going. And it all started with lack of sleep—a small decision.

Her words set me to thinking about the small decisions I make that have big consequences. If I decide I'm too busy to walk with my friend each morning, chances are I won't walk at all and that could have (literally) fatal consequences to my overall health. If I decide I'm too tired to listen to my husband, over a period of time, he might just stop sharing with me. If I harbor bitter thoughts about someone who has hurt me, I start to treat them with contempt. If I decide I don't have time to pray in the morning, I don't have the equipping I need to walk with the Lord. If I decide to skip a Bible study I've committed to attend, it becomes easier to simply stay away.

Yes, the small daily decisions of my life can certainly impact eternity.

Oh, dear Father, help me, this day, to choose to serve You—when it is convenient and when it is not. Help me to make the right choices, Lord, day after day, walking with You when it's easy and when it's hard. I choose for myself, this day, to serve You. In Jesus' Name, Amen.

GOING DEEPER
For those days when you have more time to ponder

Read Joshua 24. This is Joshua's last speech to the people of Israel. Discover what he thought was most important to share.

List some of the key points Joshua wanted the people to remember.

Review your list and add some of your own. What choices are you currently making that you need to change?

Joshua told the people to "throw away the foreign gods that are among you and yield your hearts to the Lord, the God of Israel" (Joshua 24:23). What in your life needs to be thrown away?

RESPONDING TO HIS WORD

Day 18

AND NONE OF US KNOWS

We are given no signs from God; no prophets are left, and none of us knows how long this will be. —Psalm 74:9

. . . .

Sometimes life is hard. Well, actually, life is often hard. The daily news reports one crisis after another and the future can look bleak. On a personal level, several dear ones in my life are going through really hard times: cancer, infertility, divorce, broken relationships, and more. My heart aches for each individual, and I remember times when my own heart felt like a frozen tundra with no sign of warmth or life or hope. It seemed like winter would last forever.

You know one of the hardest things about a hard time? Not knowing how long it will last. Yeah. Asaph, the writer of Psalm 74, says it very well. "We are given no signs from God; no prophets are left, and none of us knows how long this will be" (v.9).

I remember. I remember saying to God, "If only You could tell me how long I have to endure this and how it will end, I could go on with courage. I don't know whether this crisis will last another week or ten years or . . . forever. I hate this uncertainty, and I long for better days."

Reflecting on times like that, here are a few ways Asaph teaches us to cope as he wrote a heart-rending song, inspired by God, that became Bible—Psalm 74:

You might as well be honest with God. "O God, why have you rejected us forever? Why does your anger smolder against the sheep of your pasture?" Asaph laments in verse 1. You can feel his despondency, and, as is often the case with depression, the heaviness feels like it will never end. We have a tendency to walk away and sulk when God seems silent, don't we? How hard it is to open His Word when we expect disappointment! And yet, this is exactly what we must do.

Talk with God through prayer and the Word. Tell Him how you feel. Putting it into words clarifies it in our minds, and it starts the conversation with God in honesty. Asaph was great at being honestly unhappy with God!

Acknowledge that God is not doing what you want. "Why do you hold back your hand, your right hand? Take it from the folds of your garment and destroy [your foes]!" writes a frustrated Asaph in verse 11. He knew God was big enough, strong enough, mighty enough to defeat those destroying Israel, and yet he pictured God keeping His hands in His pockets. Sometimes God does not move, even when we beg Him. This is the reality. Mary and Martha begged Jesus to come heal their sick brother, and He delayed. David asked God to spare his little boy's life, and God did not. Let's not mince words. God does not always act the way we wish. He's not a genie in a bottle that we can rub and get our way. We need to acknowledge that, and still talk to Him about it.

Remember who God is and praise Him. "But God is my King from long ago; he brings salvation on the earth," Asaph admits in the very next verse. Regardless of what was going on in Asaph's world, God was still King. God was still Asaph's King. God was still the One who brings salvation to the earth. Asaph turned his eyes from the problem to the One he still trusted, despite the bleakness of his situation. If you continue reading Psalm 74, you will see how he reminds himself of God's goodness and greatness. We need to do this especially during those times when we don't see God moving. Our present difficulties do not change the innate nature of a good and loving God. Period. Faith is restored when we remember this.

Continue coming to God no matter how long it takes. "Rise up, O God, and defend your cause . . . " pleads Asaph at the end of his lament (v.22). He still asks. He still seeks. He still trusts. He goes to the only One who can fix it. Even if the fixing is taking a very long time and the wait seems interminable.

The God who created seasons will not allow a "winter" to last forever. Really. No matter how horrible your season is, dear one, it will end. One day, the temperature will shift just a bit and the ice will begin to thaw. To your amazement, green sprouts and leaves and buds of flowers will return again to the barrenness of your heart. Don't turn away from the God of all comfort! Run to Him with every thought and every feeling. Remember He is good and He loves you deeply. Keep asking and keep seeking. It won't be in vain. I think Asaph would agree.

Dear God, there are times when, like Asaph, I feel lost and alone and unmoored. I feel hurt and abandoned by You, God, even though I know that cannot be true—You are everywhere all the time. Help me in those dark times to always run to You. To trust You even when I don't feel You. To cling to You with all that's in me. And, more importantly, Lord, please cling to me. Don't let go of my hand, dear God. Walk with me each day, every day, in the good times and the bad. I need You and I want You close. In Jesus' Name, Amen.

. . . .

GOING DEEPER
For those days when you have more time to ponder

Read Psalm 74.

Choose a verse from the psalm and write it out. Turn it into a prayer for yourself or for someone you know in crisis.

If you are struggling today feeling disappointed with God in some way, write to Him, and tell Him honestly what you are thinking. He can handle it.

End your prayer time today with praise. Praise God for being Good and Merciful, for being your Savior and your Shepherd, for gifting you with eternal life, for loving you always . . . . And in that time of praise, dear one, may you discover again the joy of belonging to *Him*!

. . . .

RESPONDING TO HIS WORD

Day 19

DEVOTION

They devoted themselves to the apostles' teaching and to fellowship, to the breaking of bread and to prayer. —Acts 2:42

. . . .

My father-in-law was a man who understood devotion. This dear soul was totally devoted to his wife, my husband's beloved mother. We always said the best way to make Dad happy was to be nice to Mom. If she wanted to go shopping, he was all too happy to take her. If she forgot to pick up something at the store, out he would go at any hour of the night to buy it. If she fancied grilled pork chops in the middle of a snowy New England winter, he'd happily dig out the grill and get to work. He loved pleasing her.

When she became ill, he refused to let her be placed in a nursing home. Instead, he made all her meals, scheduled all her therapy and nursing appointments, managed all her daily medications, and completely cared for their home. How deeply he loved her. After she died, he faithfully visited her grave, bringing flowers several times a year. I've never witnessed such a boundless level of devotion in anyone else.

In Acts 2:42, we read that the followers of Jesus "devoted themselves to the apostles' teaching and to fellowship, to the breaking of bread and to prayer."

The word *devote* means "to commit wholly" and is used to describe the actions of these early believers. They committed themselves fully to the teachings of the apostles, which is now our New Testament. They were committed to other believers, to communing with them, and they were committed to prayer. Without holding anything back, these were the ways the early followers of Christ showed their devotion. How are we doing in these areas?

Am I devoted to the apostles' teaching? Do I study God's Word and ponder it? Am I making it an integral part of my daily life choices?

Am I devoted to fellowship with other believers? Do I attend a church, immersing myself in the life of the local body of Christ, serving as I can? Am I involved in a small group for prayer or Bible study where I can be real, know others and be known?

Am I "breaking bread" with other Christians? Do I know them well enough to share a meal with them? Am I fully present, remembering the Lord's death for me during the "breaking of bread" when the Lord's supper is celebrated?

Am I devoted to prayer? Do I commit wholly to speaking often with the Lord, running to Him with every need, worshiping Him with every breath?

Our world is full of wonderful activities we can devote ourselves to, many of them worthwhile. People, too, call out for our devotion—spouses, parents, children, friends. In the end, though, we all need to ask this question: Am I devoted to the One who gave me life? Does the way I spend my time reflect my wholehearted devotion to Him and His family of believers?

Francis Chan's words challenge me: "Our greatest fear should not be of failure . . . but of succeeding at things in life that don't really matter."

Oh, Father, help me to be wholly devoted to You. Forgive me when I set up an idol in Your place. You deserve to be my first Love. Help me to love others well, but to love You best. Give me a heart that yearns to study Your Word, that wants to walk with You, praying without ceasing as the day unfolds. Help me to take time to break bread and fellowship with others who love You. Give me a devoted heart. In Jesus' Name, Amen.

GOING DEEPER
For those days when you have more time to ponder

Read Acts 2:42-47 and Acts 3.

List concrete ways the disciples lived out the devotion described in Acts 2:42.

Reflect on the italicized questions in this devotional and write out your answers.

Pray for God's help in becoming more devoted to things that matter and to Him, who matters most of all.

. . . .

RESPONDING TO HIS WORD

Day 20

I CAN'T PRAY RIGHT NOW, BUT SOMEONE NEEDS TO

*He is able to save completely those who come to God through him,
because he always lives to intercede for them. —Hebrews 7:25*

I'll never forget the call I received from a neighbor. She was struggling with her marriage, and she had, again, been badly let down by her husband. Weeping and miserable and broken, she called asking me to intercede for her. With her mind too shattered to form a prayer, she reached out to me, "I can't pray right now, but someone needs to! Please pray for me."

Of course, I prayed for her, crying out on her behalf as she fought with depression and anger and bewilderment. I prayed for God's peace to descend and restore calm to her heart. I pleaded with the Lord to relieve her anxiety and hurts. I prayed for her because, at that moment, she could not.

Have you been there? Have you come alongside another in prayer? I suspect you have. That's what women of faith *do*. We join with those who are hurting and carry them before the Father's throne.

The writer of Hebrews reminds us that Jesus interceded for others during His ministry on earth and that, even today, He continues to pray! "He is able to save completely those who come to God through him, because he always lives to intercede for them" (Hebrews 7:25). What an amazing verse to ponder. Jesus intercedes for *us*. The One who created the world, spoke it into being, cares enough to pray on our behalf. Wow.

Lord Jesus, how we thank You for interceding—for us. Thank You for Your prayers for us today—and when You walked this earth many years ago. Help us to faithfully pray for others, modeling ourselves after You, Lord.

Enable us to expend the energy and emotion that is required to cry out on behalf of a broken soul. Lord, teach us how to pray—more and more. In Your Name, Amen.

. . . .

GOING DEEPER

For those days when you have more time to ponder

Read John 17.

What do you learn through this prayer about what Jesus thought was important—for His disciples and for us, the believers who have come after them?

Ask God to give you the name of someone in crisis right now. Spend time interceding for them, using Jesus' prayer in John 17 as a model where it applies.

If you still have time, pray for persecuted Christians around the globe, asking God to strengthen them.

. . . .

RESPONDING TO HIS WORD

Day 21

FLEDGLING

*Have mercy on me, my God, have mercy on me, for in you
I take refuge. I will take refuge in the shadow of your
wings until the disaster has passed. —Psalm 57:1*

· · · · · · · · · · · · · ·

Do you ever feel beaten down by relationship troubles? Or a general sadness at the state of the world? Or too many dear ones in crisis at the same time? This was right where I found myself one dreary day. Then God gently called to my mind a word picture from Psalm 91:4—His promise to cover us with His feathers and find refuge under His wings. From that picture and the following verse, a poem came to life.

Tiny bird-heart beating wildly
Tumbling in the roaring storm
Flight erratic, wings a-tremble
Searching for the safe and warm

Still and silent, great and mighty
Father watches frightened flight
Poised to rescue, eye unwavering
Keeping fledgling in His sight

Extra push with feathers trembling
Aching wings and shaking chest
Fledgling flutters toward her Father
Safety beckons 'neath His breast

Loving wings, majestic, mighty
Lift and circle round her frame
Enclosed, surrounded, warmed, protected
Nestled close He breathes her name

Battle-weary, worn and frightened
Turning toward the nest I fly
Spread Your wings and feathers o'er me
While I rest awhile and cry

Hold me close and still my trembling
Comfort me, restore my sight
Then gird me with fresh courage, boldness
To soar again in willing flight.

Dear Father, how thankful I am for You. Just the picture of You enclosing me in big, strong wings brings me peace. With You, I am safe. With You, I can rest. Keep me nestled close, dear Lord. I want to be near You always. In Your Name, Amen.

. . . .

GOING DEEPER

For those days when you have more time to ponder

Read Psalm 57.

In verse 4, David laments, "I am in the midst of lions; I am forced to dwell among ravenous beasts." Are you in a "forced" situation not of your choosing? If so, bring it before the Lord in prayer.

Notice David's honest fear expressed and his resolve to praise. Which verse resonates most with your life right now? Write it out to remember it better.

Sit still, close your eyes, and thank God that He *does* spread His wings over you, His beloved. Stay still for a bit and be thankful.

. . . .

RESPONDING TO HIS WORD

Day 22

THE DAY I THREW CEREAL BOXES ACROSS THE KITCHEN FLOOR

*Fools give full vent to their rage, but the wise
bring calm in the end. —Proverbs 29:11*

• • • • • • • • • • • • • • • •

Life is not always sunshine and sweetness around our house. Take, for example, the day I threw all the cereal boxes across the room. Yeah. That day. To begin with, I thought an aide was coming to take care of Dad's morning routine—a two-hour process. But no aide. Losing help means losing two hours out of *my* day. *Okay,* I thought. *I can do this.* I shuffled my schedule a bit, changed a phone conference call, and got to work caring for Dad. I was actually quite nice and friendly about the whole deal. My mind was racing, trying to figure out how I would make up the lost time, but my words were kind.

My day, however, didn't improve. Lunch took longer than I thought, then my work took so long that all of a sudden it was 4:00 pm, and I had no idea what to do for dinner. I took a peek into the fridge and realized there would be no dinner without a shopping trip. Off I dashed. Company was expected after dinner, so I needed to hurry. With too many groceries to unload and put away, I quickly stashed the cold items in the fridge and threw together a supper. The rest of the groceries stayed in the car. After our company left, I cleaned out the fridge, which I had earlier noticed was a total mess, and re-stacked the cold items. No time to put the dry goods away, because it was time for Ray and me to get Dad to bed.

So there I was at 10:00 pm, Dad tucked nicely in, but for me just starting to put away the rest of my groceries. First, I had to rearrange the cans cupboard to fit in the just-purchased cans, and I felt that teeny bit of patience I had barely hung onto all day definitely slipping. And then . . . the cereal . . . just would not fit. I would have to take out all the boxes and other dry goods in order to fit in the new boxes, some of which, I now could see, I hadn't actually needed to buy.

That's when I snapped. I did *not* remove cereal boxes from said cupboard. I grabbed and threw them across the floor in a wrathful display of resentment and self-pity. I shouted for my husband and demanded his help. I raged about my day and my work and wept with the misery of it all. I was pretty much a huge, big jerk.

Did you notice all the "I" statements in this tale? Yep. That day was all about poor me. My focus was not on others. My heart was not nestled in God's hands. My manufactured patience crumbled, as it always will, for on my own I have not the fortitude, nor the temperament, to be nice for very long. My anger did not produce anything good. For starters, there were now cereal boxes all over the floor, not to mention the loose cereal that had spilled out during the rampage. And, my husband had received an earful he did not need or deserve after a hard day of his own.

I wonder how differently my day might have been had I stopped right when our aide canceled—and prayed? I wonder how differently my day might have been if I had consciously asked God to carry me? Perhaps I would have been grateful to have the "problem" of too much food. Good grief! How many people in this world are hungry. Every. Single. Day. Yet I had been upset because food did not fit? Perhaps I didn't have to be the superhero and clean out cupboards on a busy day? I don't know. What I do know is that I don't do well without God. I need Him. I want Him. And He wants me—close to Him.

God cares far more about my relationship with Him and my attitude than He does about clean cupboards. He longs to be there with me on my busiest, toughest days. Staying close to Him and listening to His voice lead to the righteousness that He desires, a life of peace and blessing—for each of us and for those we touch day by day.

For this purpose Sweet Selah Ministries* was birthed: a deep desire to walk away from a life controlled by my own busy, fussy self, toward a peace-filled life controlled by God at an unhurried pace. A life in which others could join me on this journey toward more peaceful living. A life where cereal boxes stay in cupboards where they belong!

Father, forgive me when my own selfish desires make me angry and bitter. Forgive me for the many, many times I totally forget that I can cry out to You when I am in distress. Lord, my nature is to battle through and go even faster the tougher the situation.

Help me, Lord, to stop. Help me to remember that You are right here beside me, able to turn a situation. Able to calm me. Able to guide me and close my big mouth. I thank You for Your deep mercies and rich forgiveness. Oh, how grateful I am, Lord, that You never tire of hearing me confess my sins and inadequacies, and I thank You for new beginnings whenever I turn to You. I love You, Lord. In Jesus' Name, Amen.

. . . .

GOING DEEPER
For those days when you have more time to ponder

Read Proverbs 29.

Write down all that you learn about anger from this chapter of Proverbs.

Which verse do you find most convicting? Why?

Write down those situations in which you find it hard to remain calm. Look at them carefully and ask God to help you remember to cry out to Him the next time one of them arises. If you have a prayer partner, share these areas of weakness so that you can receive prayer support in overcoming them.

*Visit us online at SweetSelah.org.

. . . .

RESPONDING TO HIS WORD

Day 23

CAPTURING THOUGHTS

We demolish arguments and every pretension that sets itself up against the knowledge of God, and we take captive every thought to make it obedient to Christ. —2 Corinthians 10:5

• • • • • • • • • • • • • • • • •

I have a very active and vivid imagination. As a young mother, that imagination, combined with a habit of worry, yielded ridiculous results. If my husband, Ray, was late getting home from work, I had already imagined his traffic accident, his death, and his funeral. If my daughters had an argument, I was arranging future holiday celebrations, imagining both refusing to come to dinner with the other. Good grief. I needed to "take captive" those fearful, foolish thoughts!

Fearful thoughts were not my only struggle. Bitter thoughts rolled around in my head, as well. I resented anyone I thought had been mean to my daughters. Mix in envious thoughts, like friends whose husbands seemed to have more time for their children than mine. Oh, yes. My thought life was not a pretty place to be—a whole lot of the time.

Paul was well aware of this very human condition. He knew we'd have ugly, sinful thoughts—and he knew how dangerous they are. Jesus had clearly taught that "out of the heart come evil thoughts—murder, adultery, sexual immorality, theft, false testimony, slander" (Matthew 15:19). These sins all start in the heart, in the mind. Oh, how we *must* capture them before they take over our actions.

How do we do it? How do we take captive every thought and make it obedient to Christ? One of the best ways is to pray. Instead of imagining a fearful future, I could have prayed for Ray's safety and trusted God to look after him. I could have asked the Lord to help my girls truly love one another, instead of imagining that a single fight would result in a lifetime of enmity. Instead of bitterness, I could have prayed for the one who was mean to my girl. Perhaps that mean streak was

an indication of a deep-rooted unhappiness in her own heart. Instead of envy, I could have prayed that God would bless my husband and give him an ever-deepening love for his family.

Let's take this command seriously. When an ungodly thought enters our minds, turn it into good . . . turn it into a prayer. If we do this consistently, I can tell you from personal, happy experience, that the worried thoughts, the bitter thoughts, the envious thoughts do fade. The enemy of our souls finally realizes that popping an ungodly thought into our heads just results in more praying, and he surely does not want that. For me today, turning ungodly thoughts into godly prayers has become a habit. I love it. Try it. You will experience the double blessing—God will bless you and those for whom you are praying.

Father, help me to train my mind to turn to You. I can't do this hard thing without Your Spirit's prompting and help. Show me how to pray instead of worrying, envying, feeling bitter. Help me to always turn to You, Lord, and use me for good, not harm, in the lives of others. I ask this in the Mighty Name of Jesus, Amen.

· · · · · · · · · · · · ·

GOING DEEPER
For those days when you have more time to ponder

Read 2 Corinthians 10:1-5.

In verse 2, Paul refers to people who "think that we live by the standards of this world." List some of the standards of this world that are contrary to God's standards. For example: The world says to be strong is to be independent. God says we are to be dependent on Him.

How do we "wage war" differently than the world does?

Be proactive. What are the troubling thoughts that repeatedly invade your brain? List them and write a prayer beside each one. Ask God to help you remember to pray the next time you are attacked. May God give you victory in this area.

By the way, it took about ten months of consistently turning my bitter thoughts into prayers before they stopped. Yup. Ten. Long. Months. Don't give up. Be consistent. God will grant you success.

. . . .

RESPONDING TO HIS WORD

Day 24

SHHH! I'M HAVING MY QUIET TIME!

Very early in the morning, while it was still dark, Jesus got up, left the house and went off to a solitary place, where he prayed. —Mark 1:35

• • • • • • • • • • • • • • • • • •

It is, therefore, necessary for the Spirit of God to burn into our hearts this mystery, that the most important work we have to do is that which must be done on our knees, alone with God, away from the bustle of the world and the plaudits of men. — O. Hallesby, *Prayer*, translated by Clarence J. Carlsen

We finally put up our little screen house tent in the backyard. I love it! With a table and a lounge chair facing away from the house toward the woods, it's quiet and beautiful and the birds sing to me. A perfect spot to take my Bible and journals with my cup of tea and feel like I'm in the wilderness with God—I am filled with joy. I'm very grateful for this blessing that has come to me now that my children are grown.

For those of you who still have tiny ones, oh, don't I know how very hard it is to find a place (any place), a time (any time) to be alone with your God. Susannah Wesley, famous mother of John Wesley, used to sit in her kitchen and pop a dishtowel or apron over her head and pray—and the kids knew not to disturb her. I used to give our girls a half hour of video time in the morning while I enjoyed quiet time with God.

As difficult as it is, you need it. You need time to take a deep breath and seek God's wisdom for your day. You need His strength. You need a godly attitude. You need to remember what's important and eternal—and what's not—before your hectic day begins.

Our daughters understood the term "quiet time" early on. In fact, I remember walking into our older daughter's room when she was maybe three years old.

As I started to speak, she put a tiny finger to her lips, serious as could be, looked at me, and said, "Shhh! I having my quiet time!"

It's actually a good thing for our children to know they are not the very center of our universe. God is. When we take time to be still with Him in the midst of parenting, we model for them how very much God deserves our attention and love. I explained to our girls that I was always a nicer mommy when I had time alone with Jesus to set my heart right.

Whether you are a mom or not, look for creative ways to carve out daily time with God. Be diligent to follow the advice of O. Hallesby in the quote above and do "the most important work . . . which must be done on our knees, alone with God."

Heavenly Father, I can't live out a godly example without Your help every minute of every day. Help me to seek time alone with You in the midst of busy days. Help me to model the importance of quiet time by simply doing it. Show me the where and the when, Lord, and help me be consistent. In Jesus' Name, Amen.

· · · · · · · · · · · · · · · ·

GOING DEEPER
For those days when you have more time to ponder

Read Psalm 78. If you only have time to read part of it, we are going to focus on verses 5-7.

Reread verses 5-7. What are we commanded to do for the next generation?

List some ways you can show children, whether your own or others' children, the Word of God and the importance of knowing it and obeying it.

Ponder a good adult example from your past. What did he or she do to create in you a thirst for God? Take time to thank God for this person, and, if you are still in touch, let him/her know how grateful you are.

RESPONDING TO HIS WORD

Day 25

SPARROWS, SPARROWS EVERYWHERE

"Are not two sparrows sold for a penny? Yet not one of them will fall to the ground outside your Father's care. And even the very hairs of your head are all numbered. So don't be afraid; you are worth more than many sparrows." —Matthew 10:29-31

- - - - - - - - - - - - - - - -

I love sparrows. Have you ever noticed the way God uses the tiniest things to minister to our hearts? I remember when my husband was told he would have to retire early from the army due to a drawdown. We had expected to be in the service for at least a few more years. To make things even more difficult, we were in Germany. It's hard to apply for jobs in the United States when you're half a world away.

After much prayer, Ray decided to teach at a Christian high school if he could find a position. He has always loved history and had spent three years teaching at the United States Military Academy, so the thought of teaching history from a Christian perspective was exciting. He searched diligently for a good fit, but still working for the army and interviewing by phone made for rough going.

During this time, God drew me to Matthew 10:29-31. He reminded me that if He even notices sparrows when they fall, He certainly noticed us—and our job dilemma. It was the craziest "coincidence" . . . while we were waiting, wondering, worrying . . . I saw hundreds of sparrows . . . in likely—and unlikely—places. Whenever I started to stress, there would be a sparrow, cocking its little head at me and wondering why I was worried. I saw sparrows everywhere. And every time, God sweetly whispered, "I care for you." I still adore sparrows to this day.

God chose to let us wait and wonder about a job for a very long time. In fact, we were within two weeks of leaving Germany and still praying. As it happened, a headmaster in New Hampshire was also praying. He was looking for a strong

history teacher for a brand new Christian high school. The night after this head-master prayed on his knees for the right teacher, God reminded my sister about this job possibility and prompted her to tell us about it. Ray called the very next day, discovered that he and the headmaster had much in common, and Ray was hired on the spot. Unlike most of the other places he had looked, this job was close to our parents. So, Ray's job—that he has now enjoyed for more than two decades—was not only perfect, but we were able to live close to our dear families again. Gift, indeed!

No matter what hard time you are going through, the God who cares about the common little sparrow cares about *you*. May you see sparrows everywhere you look, and be reminded of His watchful care—even in your darkest hour.

Heavenly Father, thank You for the reminder that You are aware of every little sparrow's fall. Forgive me for the times I forget that You notice me even more. Lord, make me aware today that You are with me, and You care. Help me to see You. Help me to hear You. Enable me to obey You with joy. In Jesus' Name, Amen.

. . . .

GOING DEEPER
For those days when you have more time to ponder

Read Matthew 10.

This is not the easiest of passages. List some of the hard things Jesus says.

Why are the words in Matthew 10:26-31 so important in light of Jesus' message?

Jesus does not promise us a life of ease, does He? What He does promise is rich indeed. List the blessings He has for us based on this chapter and thank Him for each precious one.

RESPONDING TO HIS WORD

Day 26

OBEDIENT THANKS

Always be joyful. Never stop praying. Be thankful in all circumstances, for this is God's will for you who belong to Christ Jesus. —1 Thessalonians 5:16-18 NLT

. . . .

I was married for almost five years before our daughter Kathryn was born. I had wanted children much sooner, but that didn't happen. I remember visiting a friend, who had preschool children, and chatting with her in the kitchen while she was cooking. One of her little ones was in a miserable mood. She whined. She cried. She clung to her mom's leg like a little limpet making it very difficult for my friend to move. She looked at me in exasperation and blurted out, "This child is driving me crazy! I can't stand days like this!"

I tried to be sympathetic, but all I could think was, "Oh, what wouldn't I give to have a child clinging to my leg, needing me." I remember resolving right then and there that if I ever had children, I would be grateful for them every day, even on whiney, clingy, exasperating days. The day did come when I had a child in a miserable mood clinging to me, and, yes, I did remember. How I thanked my wonderful God that He made me a mother and that I had a wee one who knew she could run to me.

Today's verse teaches us that giving thanks *in all circumstances* is God's will for us. Being thankful isn't always easy, is it? At the same time, I have a feeling that cultivating a thankful heart helps us do the first part of that scripture: rejoice always. As women in America, we have so very much to be thankful for. We don't have to stand in line all day hoping there will be enough rice for our family to survive another day. We aren't huddled under a makeshift roof trying to escape the rain and wind and cold. And for those who know Christ as Lord—even if we do end up homeless and lost, longing for food and shelter, even then—we have a God who

never leaves us or forsakes us. Even then, we know that this life is very short in light of eternity spent with the King and the Shepherd who has promised us more than we can ask or imagine in the days to come.

Father, forgive me when I'm not grateful for all the plenty I have. Forgive me when I even complain about good gifts You have given me. Help me to see how much I have and to remember that always, always I have You. In Jesus' Name, Amen.

· · · · · · · · · · · · · · · · ·

GOING DEEPER
For those days when you have more time to ponder

Read 1 Thessalonians 5.

First Thessalonians 5:1-11 gives guidance on how to live in the last days. Do you ever feel like we are actually there now? Write down what you learn from Paul about how to respond in the last days.

Paul's final instructions are found in verses 12-28. List them. Study them.

Choose two or three of these instructions that you need help to do well. Write them down; ask God to help you; and, then, in obedience, give thanks for all you do have.

· · · · · · · · · · · · · · · · ·

RESPONDING TO HIS WORD

Day 27

WHAT ARE YOU WEARING TODAY?

As God's chosen people, holy and dearly loved, clothe yourselves with compassion, kindness, humility, gentleness and patience. —Colossians 3:12

- -

We all remember it as one of those days we'd like to forget. How I wish I had actively sought God that morning, asking His help in clothing myself in garb that would hold up to the strains ahead! The Colossians verse above urges us to clothe ourselves with compassion, kindness, humility, gentleness, and patience. That must mean it doesn't come naturally—I know it doesn't always for me—I have to put them on like a garment.

The particular day that lives on in infamy in the annals of the Gamble family happened when we lived in Germany and I was home schooling our children. Most days, I loved it and relished the time with my girls. On this day, however, my mind was not on school or on my daughters. I had a different agenda: finish quickly so I could join friends for lunch. I was feeling lonely and opportunities to meet friends were rare. My heart was set on going, but first we needed to get through school. All morning I prodded and pushed, impatient with their questions, as it became more and more apparent that I would either have to leave schoolwork undone (something I had committed not to do) or miss my lunch.

I finally exploded at one of my poor little girls over her spelling lesson, and we both erupted in tears with her sister joining us in sympathy and anxiety. My harsh words had lasting repercussions in my daughter's life, and I learned a hard lesson: the vital importance of clothing myself with compassion. Selfishness is never the right outfit to wear. It's ugly and crass and never fits well.

Compassion, on the other hand, feels the distress of another, has pity. If I had been clothed in compassion instead of self, I would have noticed my girls' stress levels, provoked by me. I would have sensed their pain and seen that my impatience was making them feel inept and unloved. Oh, how I dislike remembering that day!

How very thankful I am that our God is a God of compassion. He feels our hurts and woes. He has pity on us. He notices us in our distress. He is perfect Love. I want to be more like Him in what I wear each day.

How do we clothe ourselves with compassion, kindness, humility, gentleness, and patience? We spend time with Him. The best way to become like someone is to spend time in their presence. (That's why we're concerned about the friends our children make.) May we be faithful to spend time with God each day in our own homes and together with others in worship and study and prayer. When I start the day in His Word and prayer, I remember the goodness of my God and am quieted in His Presence. He calms me and clothes me with the compassion and those other qualities I so need. I'm forever grateful for this incredible access to the living God. Oh, how I need to start each morning at His feet, "dressing" myself in clothing that can stand up to the wear and tear that will be an inevitable part of my day.

Father God, how I need You. Help me, please, not to rush into this day or any day. Clothe me. Show me how to dress myself with Your compassion for those who are hurting. Remind me to treat everyone I meet with kindness, realizing that I don't know their full story, and help me to give them grace. Father, may I humble myself to do the small and lowly tasks and to lift You high, not myself. Help me to applaud others' achievements without boasting of my own. Keep me gentle, Lord, especially with my immediate family. Help me to speak words I won't regret. Give me Your patient love as I serve others this day. In all I do, Lord, may my life reflect You. In Your Name, Jesus, and trusting in Your strength, Amen.

. . . .

GOING DEEPER
For those days when you have more time to ponder

Read Colossians 3.

95

This passage is full of practical guidance. List at least 10 pieces of wise counsel from Paul in this chapter.

As you ponder "clothing yourself with compassion, kindness, humility, gentleness, and patience," what is the hardest trait for you to "put on"? Why?

Write out a prayer, asking God for His help in "getting dressed" today. If another verse from this chapter convicts you, pray for His help in that area as well.

· · · · · · · · · · · · · · ·

RESPONDING TO HIS WORD

Day 28

WHEN YOU DON'T KNOW HOW TO PRAY

"This, then, is how you should pray: 'Our Father in heaven, hallowed be your name, your kingdom come, your will be done, on earth as it is in Heaven.'" —Matthew 6:9-10

· · · · · · · · · · · · · · · · ·

Have you ever wondered how to pray about a situation when you see good people on both sides of the issue, and you simply don't understand which side God would take?

Watchman Nee was a brilliant thinker, church leader, Christian teacher, and author who worked in China in the 20th century. As he watched a conflict between Japan and his homeland of China, his prayer was not for one country or the other, but for God's agenda.

The Lord reigns; we affirm it boldly. Our Lord Jesus Christ is reigning, and he is Lord of all; nothing can touch His authority. It is spiritual forces that are out to destroy His interests in China and Japan. Therefore we do not pray for China; we do not pray for Japan; but we pray for the interests of thy Son in China and Japan. We do not blame any men, for they are only tools in the hand of thine enemy. We stand for thy will. Shatter, O Lord, the kingdom of darkness, for the persecutions of thy church are wounding thee. Amen.
— Watchman Nee, Prayer at Keswick Convention, England, 1938

Joshua had a most interesting encounter with the commander of the army of the Lord, who many commentators believe to be a pre-incarnate Jesus. In Joshua 5:13-15 we read:

Now when Joshua was near Jericho, he looked up and saw a man standing in front of him with a drawn sword in his hand. Joshua went up to him and asked, "Are you for us or for our enemies?"

"Neither," he replied, "but as commander of the army of the Lord I have now come." Then Joshua fell facedown to the ground in reverence, and asked him, "What message does my Lord have for his servant?"

The commander of the Lord's army replied, "Take off your sandals, for the place where you are standing is holy." And Joshua did so.

Notice that this commander did not take sides from a human perspective. God's focus and plans are far bigger than ours and bigger than any nation's plans. Like Joshua, sometimes we just need to take off our sandals in awe at His holiness.

As you and I pray today for complex problems in the world and perhaps in our own families, let us always pray for the interests of God's Son. Let us always stand for God's will and ask God to shatter the kingdom of darkness. To pray that God's will be done is to model our Lord's prayer in the garden, "Father, if you are willing, take this cup from me; yet not my will, but yours be done" (Luke 22:42).

Lord, so often I do not know how to pray. I don't know what Your will is in a situation, or I don't have all the facts to make decisions. But this I do know: You reign. You are sovereignly in charge of all that happens. Guide me as I pray to focus on what will bring You glory and what will further Your kingdom here on earth. In Jesus' Mighty Name, Amen.

· · · · · · · · · · · · · ·

GOING DEEPER
For those days when you have more time to ponder

Read Matthew 6.

Take time as you read to actually *pray* the Lord's Prayer in Matthew 6:9-13.

What do you learn about worry from this chapter?

List two or three of the most complex problems you are facing or our world is facing. Following Watchman Nee's example, pray about these problems from the perspective of God's will that "every knee should bow ... and every tongue acknowledge that Jesus Christ is Lord" (Philippians 2:10b-11a).

RESPONDING TO HIS WORD

Day 29

KNOWN BY GOD

"Before I formed you in the womb I knew you." —Jeremiah 1:5a

. . . .

I find it amazing that two daughters raised in the same home with the same parents fifteen months apart with almost identical experiences could be so very different. Our girls are both wonderful women, but each is truly unique.

One is a working woman with a son, a foster son, a couple of side jobs, and a gift for juggling a multitude of tasks. The foster children she takes in could not have a better advocate, as she makes sure each one receives what they need to flourish. Our other daughter is a homeschooling mom, who loves cooking and baking and mentoring younger moms. She thrives on and is grateful for the stay-at-home lifestyle. I'm very proud of both of them. But, whoa. They are different.

I suspect you have observed this same trend in your siblings or children. God created each one of us uniquely—and He knows us from the very beginning of our existence. He knows our inmost being. As I write, a little one is forming in my younger daughter's womb. God has planned his or her personality and character traits and wired them into the DNA.

Think about it for a moment . . . this is one huge reason we can pray with confidence. God *knows* our hearts. He sees our aches and how our past has shaped our present. God *knows* the hearts of our loved ones, far better than we do. He knows how they are wired. He knows their gifts, their strengths, their weaknesses, their fears. He knows how to help them and heal them and equip them to do His will. He *understands* our spouse!

When we come to Him in prayer for our family, our friends . . . our enemies, we are bringing them before the One who knows them better than they know themselves. Paul says that, "we are God's handiwork, created in Christ Jesus" (from Ephesians 2:10). Take joy in knowing how much God loves you and yours. We can freely talk to Him about any individual with great confidence that He already knows them intimately.

Oh, Lord, You have searched me, and You know me for You created my inmost being (Psalm 139:1, 13). Thank You that You care deeply for me and for mine. Father, as I come to You today in prayer for my dear ones, thank You for the assurance that You know them. Help me to trust that You know what is best for them. In Jesus' Name, Amen.

· · · · · · · · · · · · · ·

GOING DEEPER
For those days when you have more time to ponder

Read Psalm 23.

List a few people you have a burden for today, and write down their greatest needs from your perspective.

One by one, place their names into Psalm 23, praying: Lord, You are _____'s Shepherd. Help him/her realize he/she doesn't need to be in want. He/She has You to provide the peace of green pastures and still waters . . .

If your loved one does not know God, pray: Lord, help _____ recognize that You are the true Shepherd. Show him/her that everything he/she wants and needs is found in You.

Finish by praying this psalm for yourself, thanking your Shepherd for His great love for you even before you were first formed in your mother's womb.

· · · · · · · · · · · · · ·

RESPONDING TO HIS WORD

Day 30

WRESTLING IN PRAYER

Epaphras, who is one of you and a servant of Christ Jesus, sends greetings. He is always wrestling in prayer for you, that you may stand firm in all the will of God, mature and fully assured. —Colossians 4:12

Epaphras, a man mentioned in the verse above, must have been quite a guy. He didn't just pray, he "wrestled" in prayer. This interesting word caught my attention. Just what does it mean? How do I wrestle in prayer? One commentary I checked translated it, "wrestling in agony of prayer" (Charles Ellicott). Another said, "properly denotes contending, or combating in the games; here it signifies the greatest fervency of desire and affection in prayer" (Joseph Benson). This is heavy duty prayer. Doesn't sound fun. In fact, it sounds like a lot of work. Yet . . . sometimes . . . we need to pray with that kind of labor and intensity.

Just like we have all kinds of conversations, our prayers, too, won't all be the same. When I talk with my husband, sometimes we discuss mundane, repetitive things like, "What time will you be home?" "Did you pay the electric bill?" Sometimes we discuss deep things like, "Did you understand what the pastor was saying in his sermon?" Sometimes we wrestle—"How should we respond appropriately to slander spoken against us?"

Part of an intimate relationship is interacting on many levels. Prayer gives us that opportunity with the Lord. Sometimes our prayers are routine, "Father, give my friend a happy day." Sometimes they're deeper, "Lord, I don't understand this scripture." Sometimes we wrestle.

Wrestle is an intense word that implies a conflict, a struggle, contending, grappling. What was Epaphras wrestling about in prayer? He wanted the Colossians to "stand firm in all the will of God, mature and fully assured." They, like us, were prone to fickleness. We get excited about something and pursue it with great gusto at first,

but then, the excitement wanes, and the hard work of persevering begins. Epaphras didn't want the people of his church to waver or falter. He wanted that so badly that he wrestled in his prayers, pleading with God to help them stand firm. Now *that* is worth praying with fervor. Oh, that we might all stand firm, mature and fully assured that our God *is* God and that *He* is our firm foundation. Oh, that we might all be willing to wrestle in prayer!

Father, help me to willingly enter this battlefield of prayer for my family and for my church, that in these dark days we would stand firm on the truths of Your Word and Your unchanging Goodness. Protect us from the enemy who would wean us away from what is true and good. Help us to stand firm in all Your will, mature and fully assured that You are the way, the truth, and the life, and that no one comes to You except through Your Son, Jesus. It's in His Name we pray, Amen.

. . . .

GOING DEEPER

For those days when you have more time to ponder

Read Ephesians 6:10-20.

Make a note of every mention of prayer in this passage.

What can you learn about wrestling in prayer from these verses?

What prevents you from doing the hard work of wrestling in prayer? Is God prompting you to labor in prayer for someone? Take time right now, dear one, and battle for them in prayer.

. . . .

RESPONDING TO HIS WORD

Day 31

CELEBRATING ABUNDANT LIFE

I came that they may have and enjoy life, and have it in abundance (to the full, till it overflows). —John 10:10b AMPC

• • • • • • • • • • • • • • • •

I remember holding our girls in my arms when they were babies as if it were yesterday. I remember feeling amazed at the love that welled up in me as I gazed at them. I just couldn't seem to get enough of their sweet, little faces. When someone asked to hold them, it was hard for me to give them up even for a few minutes. Perhaps it was the long wait before having children or perhaps it was simply the wonder of seeing brand new life, but in any case, I was smitten. I wanted (and still want) nothing but the best for my girls—and now for their families as well.

That is the same longing our God has for us! Jesus says in the verse above that He came that we might have life in all its fullness. He loves us, like mothers and fathers love their children—only more. He lavishes love on us (1 John 3:1). He counts the hairs on our heads (Matthew 10:30). Who but a doting parent would do that? He quiets us with His love and rejoices over us with singing (Zephaniah 3:17). He gives us instructions on how to live so we may truly live life to the fullest, and He has work for us to do that will be fulfilling and rewarding (Ephesians 2:10).

God has the same love and delight and concern for our loved ones. He, too, wants the best for them. As we come to Him in prayer today, let's be thankful for the abundant, new life He gives to all who "receive him, to those who [believe] in his name, he [gives] the right to become children of God" (John 1:12). Let's praise Him for being the life-giver and the parent who dearly loves us—and all the little (and not-so-little) ones. He gave His life that we might have life . . . abundantly.

Father, forgive me when I doubt that You came to give me an abundant life. Help me to trust that You truly do love me that much.

Thank You that You count the hairs on my head. Thank You that You want to quiet me with Your love and that You rejoice over me with singing. Thank You for having a plan and a purpose for me. Give me a deep understanding that I may live in the abundance of Your love. In Jesus' Name, Amen.

GOING DEEPER
For those days when you have more time to ponder

Read John 10:1-21.

Write down all you learn about who Jesus is from these verses.

If you have received Jesus as your Savior, what do each of these characteristics mean in your life? (If you haven't, see "If I Could Tell You Just One Thing" on page 22.)

Spend time rereading this passage, praying as you go, thanking God for Jesus, the Good Shepherd, God-in-flesh, our Savior.

RESPONDING TO HIS WORD

Day 32

WHEN YOU DON'T LIKE THE STORY

Consider it pure joy, my brothers and sisters, whenever you face trials of many kinds, because you know that the testing of your faith produces perseverance. . . . Blessed is the one who perseveres under trial because, having stood the test, that person will receive the crown of life that the Lord has promised to those who love him. —James 1:2-3, 12

. . . .

I'm thinking back to a time when both our daughters were struggling. They were often angry with me and with each other—and I had no idea how the story of our lives together would end. Comparing my life to a book, I was in the middle of a very long and dismal chapter, and, quite frankly, I wanted a rewrite.

Yet, the Bible is clear that we are to thank God in all circumstances. James even goes so far as to say that we can count it pure joy when we face trials. Here are some of the lessons God taught me about living in gratitude during that hard time:

How easy it is to praise God when all is going well. How much more strongly we show our love for Him by giving Him our praise when our lives are a mess. Turning to God in sorrow and distress and trusting Him still is a gift of faith we offer. And, such a costly gift can be counted as joy.

Studying the book of Jeremiah taught me how intensely God suffered when His children, the Israelites, rejected Him. I was drawn close to Him, knowing He truly felt and understood my pain.

Trials drove me to cry out to God over and over for our children. Because of hardship, I experienced a passion and a closeness to Him for which I am deeply grateful.

God's love surrounded me and gave me a calm assurance that I was not alone. Even in the midst of heartache, I had One who held my hand. I was still His child. No matter what.

God had the opportunity to teach me about unconditional love. (How hard it is to pour out love on one who is acting unlovely!) The life lessons and character lessons He taught me during that time . . . I needed then, and I need today.

I rediscovered the vital importance of spending time with Him each day. Without that time, it is impossible to cope in a godly way.

I clung to my Moms in Prayer group.* When my faith was weak, those other moms had faith on my behalf. They loved me, and they loved my children through prayer. I treasure the gifts of faith and love and time they invested in praying for my children.

Today, in my "book of life," I find myself in a happier chapter. As I look back at all the miracles, big and small, that God has worked in me and in my loved ones, I stand in amazement. But I know that in this world of sin and uncertainty at any moment a happy chapter can turn into a dark one. Still, I can rest in absolute certainty, that, if and when troubled times come, God will be right there with me. Of that, I have no doubt.

Father, I am exceedingly grateful You know the beginning to the end. Nothing is hidden from Your eyes. Where I see a mess, You see the beginnings of victory. Where I see failure, You see new strength rising out of the brokenness. Help me, Lord, to trust You with my story all the days of my life. Thank You that I know the ending—and it is very good. I yield to You, Lord, and trust You to guide me through every chapter, the happy ones and the sad ones. How I praise You for Jesus and the true story of redemption through His shed blood for me. I am forever thankful and pray in His Name, Amen.

GOING DEEPER
For those days when you have more time to ponder

Read James 1.

What verse resonates most with you today? Why?

What trials are you enduring right now? How are you doing at "counting it all joy"? What good can you find in the midst of the trial? List everything God brings to mind.

Take time to thank God for your story—your life. Thank Him for good times and hard times and remember that He holds you at all times.

*Moms in Prayer International is an organization that brings mothers and grandmothers together once a week to pray for the lives of their children, their grandchildren, and their teachers and schools. For more information, visit MomsInPrayer.org.

. . . .

RESPONDING TO HIS WORD

Day 33

THE DAY SHAUNDRA SPOKE UP

"If you do away with the yoke of oppression, with the pointing finger and malicious talk, and if you spend yourselves in behalf of the hungry and satisfy the needs of the oppressed, then your light will rise in the darkness, and your night will become like the noonday." —Isaiah 58:9b–10

. . . .

I can't remember her name. It was something soft and beautiful . . . like Shaundra. She was gentle and beautiful, too, soft like her name. Always a smile on her face, she did her work in my Christian middle school English classroom with intelligence and wit. I enjoyed her, and, after class whenever time allowed, I loved to chat with her. I simply assumed she was as happy as she seemed, and it never occurred to me to look deeper. As a second-year teacher, young and very naïve, I had no idea this bright, young girl was being mocked, bullied, and harassed.

In the late fall that school year, Shaundra asked me about an upcoming oral report. She wanted to do her report on prejudice, even though it wasn't on my list of suggestions. "Sure," I said, knowing that whatever she presented would be thoughtful and good. I looked forward to hearing it. Oral reports were always a nice break from teaching, sitting in the back of the classroom, listening for a change, and evaluating students in their public speaking skills.

I was pretty relaxed when Shaundra's name was called and took out my sheet to start taking notes. Almost immediately, I realized this oral presentation was not like the others. She stood straight and tall, spoke clearly with great determination, and she directed her words to one certain young man. Although I never saw his face, his neck soon became bright, mottled red, and his head was down on his desk. He never once looked up despite the fact that Shaundra's eyes were focused on him, and only him, the entire time she spoke.

I can't recall her exact words after so many years, but she said something close to this: "My father is black and my mother is white. They met in college, fell in love, and they have the happiest marriage I have ever seen. I'm their only child, and they love me. We are a close family, and we enjoy vacations together and laughing and watching movies. We pray together and go to church together and my parents show the love of Jesus to me and to others. I am tired of being mocked and bullied because of the color of my skin. My parents are the finest people I know, and I am so proud I belong to them and so proud that I look like both of them. For those of you who can't understand that, I feel sorry for you. You don't know the kind of love I've grown up with."

There was more, but you get the idea. I could still weep with pride and awe that this 14-year-old girl had the poise and the confidence to speak truth to her classmates. She spoke as she always did with her beautiful, soft voice—and the classroom was stiller than still. Her voice was clearly heard as everyone froze and listened, knowing this was Shaundra's stand against her tormentor. The applause at the end was as loud as the room had been quiet. We clapped and clapped our hands raw. The young man who had been cruel kept his head down.

Afterwards, I talked with Shaundra and learned the ways he had tormented her. I spoke to him and his parents, and our class seemed to go back to normal again. But as I look back, from the perspective of age and sad experience, I realize that I did not do enough. I should have checked in with her often to make sure all was well. I should have watched and listened more intently. Because I was not a target, I was not as aware as I should have been that someone else was.

Shaundra, if you read these words one day, please forgive me for not following up and doing more. I sincerely hope you have found a good man like your dad and that you are living a full and loving life with him. You are loved, dear girl, and I still feel weepy even today remembering your bravery in that classroom long, long ago. Well done, dear one, well done.

Father, forgive me when I insulate myself from the hard things. I confess that sometimes I'd much rather not know than deal with prejudice and oppressors. Help me to speak up when I see unkindness and worse. Lord, help me to call evil . . . evil.

Help me to help those who mock to see the harm they cause and the foolishness of their mocking. Help me to stand beside those who endure mocking and feel it with them. Teach me, Lord, to love as You love. In Jesus' Name, Amen.

· · · · · · · · · · · · · · ·

GOING DEEPER
For those days when you have more time to ponder

Read Isaiah 58.

God is angry about the way His people are fasting. Why?

List the ways described in this chapter that God wants us to serve and help those less fortunate.

Pray. Do you know any individuals who might be hurting and harassed like Shaundra? Ask God what action He would have you take to help them. Ask Him to give you eyes to see the needs around you.

· · · · · · · · · · · · · · ·

RESPONDING TO HIS WORD

Day 34

ACTUALLY KNOWING GOD

This is what the LORD says: "Let not the wise boast of their wisdom or the strong boast of their strength or the rich boast of their riches, but let the one who boasts boast about this: that they have the understanding to know me, that I am the LORD, who exercises kindness, justice and righteousness on earth, for in these I delight," declares the LORD. —Jeremiah 9:23-24

It still stuns me. The One who created the Universe, who holds the stars in His hands . . . wants to know *me*. According to the verses above, God says that of all I possess, the most important is the understanding to *know Him*. He values that ability more than any wisdom, strength, or riches I may have. In fact, He'd like me to boast about this ability to know Him, if I'm of a mind to boast. I have His permission to brag about knowing Him, the living God. Seriously. What could be better than that? What could compare with knowing the King of kings?

I love these verses from Jeremiah—and all that God has taught me through memorizing and reflecting on them. I invite you to take a "Selah" pause and ponder them with me:

Don't boast about yourself. "This is what the LORD says: 'Let not the wise boast of their wisdom or the strong boast of their strength or the rich boast of their riches'" (Jeremiah 9:23). Let's face it. God made us. If we have wisdom, it's because He gave it to us. If we are strong of body, we have Him to thank. Illness and disease can strike at any time; whatever strength we have is a gift from God. If we happen to be rich, we best not boast about that either. Stock markets crash. Earthquakes wipe out businesses. Banks fail. Without God, no rich man succeeds. Skill, knowledge, good fortune? Every good gift we enjoy is from the hand of God. The proper response is thankfulness.

Boast about God. "But let the one who boasts boast about this: that they have the understanding to know me" (Jeremiah 9:24a). Our God is amazing! Let's not be shy about telling others what He means to us. Everyone who has turned his life over to God can attest to the fact that He changes us and helps us. In strength and in weakness, in riches and in poverty, in good times and in troubled times, our God is always there. That's worth boasting about.

God is perfect. "'I am the LORD, who exercises kindness, justice and righteousness on earth, for in these I delight,' declares the LORD" (Jeremiah 9:24b). God is the perfect parent, blending kindness toward us out of His deep love, along with justice and righteousness that are necessary for us to grow in goodness and knowledge of truth. Kindness deteriorates into weakness when it's not partnered with justice and righteousness. God is perfect in His qualities and attributes, and we can *rest* in that. How wonderful that God *delights* in showing us kindness, justice, and righteousness. God enjoys being God! That's fun to contemplate.

Father, thank You for the understanding You give me to know You. God of Heaven and Earth, You reign above all things. You are beyond our comprehension, and yet You invite us to know You. Lord, let this be our heart's desire. To know You who made us and love us . . . and to know You more and more. In Jesus' Name, Amen.

GOING DEEPER
For those days when you have more time to ponder

Read Job 38-42:3. A long passage, but try to read it all if time permits.

Write down what you learn about God from His own description of Himself.

Why do you think God chose to answer Job's complaints with a description of who He is rather than an explanation of why bad things had happened to Job?

What are some concrete ways you intend to know God better this year? Thank Him that He has given you the understanding to know Him.

RESPONDING TO HIS WORD

Day 35

BITTER ROOTS

See to it that no one falls short of the grace of God and that no bitter root grows up to cause trouble and defile many. —Hebrews 12:15

• • • • • • • • • • • • • • •

It was not an easy time. My husband, Ray, had been invited by West Point, his alma mater, to attend graduate school, all expenses paid, and then to teach at the United States Military Academy. In fact, if he wished, he could get a master's degree—*and* his doctorate. At the time, it seemed like a no-brainer. I mean. Wow. Free PhD? How cool was that?

It wasn't until we were too far into the decision to back out, that we realized "free" wasn't exactly . . . free. God blessed us with two little girls just 15 months apart, and our second arrived during those two years Ray was in grad school. I juggled two in diapers while he juggled extra courses. We had a great church and support system and somehow it was working, even though we both felt a bit frazzled and disconnected from each other. Yet . . . as I handled the household alone and soldiered on, tiny little roots of bitter discontent began popping up in my brain.

Then Ray became a professor at West Point *and* writer of a dissertation—and that's when life became unbearable for both of us. Ray had to leave early in the morning and drive half an hour to West Point. He'd return home and go directly to his office to create lesson plans, grade papers, and write another chapter in his dissertation. He ate with us . . . barely . . . normally without speaking and returned to his office until bedtime. He was always exhausted and always felt behind. I wish I could say I was the super understanding wife, but that would be a bald-faced lie.

I was home all day with preschoolers, paying the bills, running the household, and caring for our two tinies—all without assistance from my overworked husband. It felt like this cycle of overwork was never going to end. I was convinced I had married a workaholic and was destined to basically single-parent for life—and the bitterness began to grow.

Then, I allowed my thoughts to drift into comparison mode. My neighbors' husbands had chosen to settle for master's degrees and a life. One husband could be seen from my window playing with his daughters on the hammock in the early evenings while mine raced through his grading alone in his office. The other neighbor's husband was famous for taking his little girl on a Saturday morning date. I'd watch her in a pretty little frilled dress walking hand in hand with her daddy week after week. It hurt. And my bitterness grew and started to choke out any remaining joy. When Ray finally had a small chance to come up for air and talk to me, he was given an angry earful about how poorly he was doing as a husband. *That* didn't exactly encourage him to want to spend more time with me.

The author of Hebrews warns against a "bitter root"—and that is a perfect picture of what happens. Roots entwine to uphold their plant or tree, and the longer that plant is around, the more entrenched the roots become and the harder to pull them out. My bitterness had become entrenched. When I saw the kindness of other husbands, my heart immediately went to bitterness and that ugly root grew a bit deeper. Our home was a most unhappy place, and I became an ugly, unhappy person. I started to dislike *me*. A lot.

At this point, I actually cried out for help. I called a wise pastor's wife, who didn't spare me with platitudes and agreement. She warned me about that entrenched root and told me it had to go before it killed me—and my marriage. She challenged me to turn every bitter thought into a prayer for my husband's well-being. *What?* That was, of course, the last thing on earth I wanted to do! But I was desperate—and it was obvious that bitterness was wrong, evil, and suffocating. So, painful uprooting began.

Each time I felt bitter, I prayed. I prayed that Ray would love God with all his heart and soul and mind. I prayed that Ray would love his family . . . us . . . more and more. I asked God to bless and help him. When I saw one of the other husbands at the window, I turned and prayed for mine. It took time. It was hard. It took discipline and encouragement from my mentor. But slowly, prayer by prayer, that bitter root was unearthed . . . exposed . . . and cut off. The plant of bitterness in my life began to fade, and my happiness made a comeback *even though* our circumstances had not changed.

Ray and I are still married, these many years later. How thankful I am for my mentor's wise advice and for God's Word that cautioned me to "see to it that no one falls short of the grace of God [oh, how my husband needed grace from

me and not condemnation!] and that no bitter root grows up to cause trouble and defile many" (Hebrews 12:15).

I shudder to think what would have happened if I had allowed that root to continue growing unchecked. I suspect it would have caused major trouble, and we likely would have divorced. I would have missed out on a wonderful marriage with a man who has grown closer and closer to me in love and tenderness with each passing year. Our children would have been "defiled" by that bitterness and robbed of their daddy. Our ability to serve God might have been severely hindered.

God's Word is true. His commands are for our good. If you are growing a bitter root in your own life against someone, take it from one who has been there. With God's help: *Rip. It. Out.* Turn those thoughts into prayers for that someone. *No matter how hard it is!* Are you thinking, "It's already too late for me?" It's *never* too late to ask for His help. It's *never* too late to rip out those bitter roots. It's *never* too late to forgive, even if your marriage is not saved, even if a friendship is not redeemed. Life is far worse when we ignore God's wise instruction and allow bitterness to grow.

Heavenly Father, thank You for Your Word. Help me to notice the bitter roots in my life. Show me where the beginnings are so I can turn from those thoughts to prayer. Show me the massive root of bitterness, Lord, if there is one. Give me courage to surrender it to You. Show me how, Lord! It is too hard for me, but nothing is too difficult for You. I ask that You help me live a life of love. Always. And thank You, Lord, for Your great, undeserved, merciful love for me. It's because of Jesus and in His Name that I pray, Amen.

. . . .

GOING DEEPER
For those days when you have more time to ponder

Read Hebrews 12.

This is a chapter full of challenge. What challenges you most in these verses?

Ponder the story of Esau, who gave away his birthright, and then suffered from bitterness and regret. If you have time, read it again in Genesis 25:29-34. Can you think of a time in your life when a "bitter root" sprang up from a situation of your own making? Ouch. Thank God for His forgiveness, if you've asked for it. If you have not, confess it now and receive God's forgiveness—then thank Him.

Pause for a moment and ask God if there is someone in your life about whom it's easy to become bitter. Ask God for a scripture or godly words you can pray for him or her. Covenant with God to pray for that person, using that scripture or those words all this week. At least.

* * * * * * * * * * * * * * * *

RESPONDING TO HIS WORD

Day 36

EGGS IN A BASKET

Above all else, guard your heart, for everything you do flows from it. —Proverbs 4:23

· · · · · · · · · · · · · · ·

Sometimes life can seem overwhelming and there just doesn't seem to be anyone who can help. Ever been there? I shared in yesterday's devotion, "Bitter Roots," about a time in my marriage when I felt very alone. My husband was busy with work and a dissertation and had no spare time or energy for a wife whose emotions were as fragile as eggs. It seemed like every time I shared a hurt or emotional need with him, he just "dropped the egg." Splat. And I had a whole basketful. To be fair, he was exhausted, and I was needy. Not a good combination.

A wise mentor taught me to turn my bitter thoughts into prayers—and she helped me see that I could not, in this season, depend on my husband to safely carry my emotions. He just couldn't do it. In fact, if I'd had more maturity, I could have helped *him* in *his* time of need. But I was too wrapped up in my own needs to see his.

So . . . what do you do when you are emotionally fragile and your "go to" person is "gone"? It's important that "above all else, guard your heart, for everything you do flows from it" (Proverbs 4:23).

What if, during that time of emotional neediness, I had befriended a kind man? Oh, what a disaster that would have been! We must be so very careful to guard our hearts from the wrong kind of help. When we are emotionally vulnerable, our walls have to be up extra high against the temptations that come.

What if, I had turned to ungodly counsel? *What if* I had listened to women who urged me toward resentment? *What if* I had sought out vapid sympathy when I needed truth?

So . . . where do we go with our emotional "eggs"?

To God Himself. That I had to depend on God for help and not on a human being was actually good. Through time in His Word and days of crying out to Him, a relationship was forged that was far stronger than it would have been had a human being pampered me and met all my needs. Still, God blessed me with . . .

A counselor/mentor. I thank God that I took my complaints to someone bold and godly. How blessed I was with a woman wise enough to point me to Christ. Someone who reminded me to focus on all the blessings I did have. Someone who spoke truth to me—the truth that I had a God who loves me; that I had a roof over my head and plenty to eat; that I had two wonderful, healthy little girls who filled my life with joy; and that I had a husband who worked very hard to provide for us so that I could stay home with them.

A solid Bible study group. I'm eternally grateful for my group during that time of loneliness. The study kept me in the Word, where I was reminded of *who* God is and *whose* I am. Spending time with individuals who knew and loved God helped me remember where to turn. Listening to their prayers reminded me to pray.

Are you feeling fragile? Don't let hard times be a way the enemy gains a foothold in your life and tries to bring you down. Remember that God is always able to hold you, always available to listen, to counsel, to love. He is never too busy. Never in a hurry. And He knows your needs before you even ask Him.

Heavenly Father, thank You that You are always near. How grateful I am that You provide a safe place for me to run when I feel fragile. Forgive me, Lord, when I expect humans—even good ones—to meet all my needs. Help me to always guard my heart. It's Yours, Lord. Help me to be wise in times of loneliness. Help me always to run toward You. In Jesus' Name, Amen.

. . . .

GOING DEEPER
For those days when you have more time to ponder

Read Proverbs 4.

What does Solomon have to say about wisdom in this chapter?

List five great nuggets of truth you gleaned.

Choose one of the five and pray for yourself and for your loved ones that you can put this proverb into practice.

. . . .

RESPONDING TO HIS WORD

Day 37

I AM NOT THE HERO

And my God will meet all your needs according to his glorious riches in Christ Jesus. To our God and Father be glory for ever and ever. Amen. —Philippians 4:19–20

. . . .

A dear friend of mine has breast cancer. Discovered this past spring, it came as quite a shock. She lives alone and has very few people she can call on for help. I have always been one of those people, but this spring . . . I was not there for her. And the distress I felt about that was immense.

At the time, I was going through my own struggles. Finishing up my term as national director of a nonprofit ministry while caregiving for my father-in-law didn't leave enough hours in the day to even do both those jobs well. Added to that were other family responsibilities and needs . . . and I was pretty close to exhaustion. I emailed my friend occasionally to ask how she was doing, but lived with a sense of guilt knowing I'd been no help. Some days, Satan had a field day in my mind. I felt so guilty for not being there. I made her no meals. I seldom called. I drove her to no appointments.

This summer, I had more free time but was reluctant to connect with my friend, knowing I had, in my mind, failed her. Finally, when I wrote and apologized for how little I had done and asked how I could help, she wrote back listing all the ways others had jumped in. Neighbors were bringing meals and hanging out with her. Her boss had been generous with time off. Church friends had come by to pray with her and drive her to appointments. She was actually . . . fine.

And then it hit me. I don't have to be the hero. In fact, I'm not *supposed* to be the hero. *God* is the one who supplies every need—and He called on other members of His body to reach out to her. This particular crisis didn't have my name on it. Oh, dear. I suddenly realized the enemy had snookered me. I had listened to the

one the Bible calls "the accuser" (Revelation 12:10). I had fallen for his lies about my own importance in my friend's situation.

She didn't need *me*. She needed *God*. The real hero. And God showed up in the hands and feet of His people, chosen by Him to meet her needs. How much time and energy I had wasted inside my brain as I lamented my inability to help. How much better it would have been had I simply laid her needs before the Lord, sought Him for what He would have me do—or not do—and then put my hands and feet to the work God *had* called me to do.

Paul understood perfectly when he wrote the Philippians, "I rejoice greatly in the Lord that at last you have renewed your concern for me. Indeed, you have been concerned, but you had no opportunity to show it" (Philippians 4:10). My friend was not angry with me, but rather was excited to share how God was meeting her needs. As I saw what He was doing, I rejoiced with her—and repented of my self-centered "need" to be her personal hero. God knew my situation this spring, knew I had no opportunity to help, and He asked others. Simple as that.

Forgive me, Lord, for prideful thinking—that I have to be the one to save people. Help me to hear Your voice clearly, helping whenever You call me, but not wallowing in false guilt when You have chosen others. Oh, how I need to recognize Your voice, Lord, so I do not live under condemnation from the enemy of my soul. Thank You for meeting my friend's needs. Thank You that You are more than able to meet all our needs according to Your glorious riches. You, Father, are the hero. Always. I bow before You in Jesus' Name, Amen.

. . . .

GOING DEEPER
For those days when you have more time to ponder

Read Philippians 4.

List at least 10 practical commands from God found in this chapter.

Which one is the hardest for you to follow? Ask for God's help in obeying.

Is there a situation in your life in which you are trying to do the "saving" when you need to step out of the way instead? If so, talk to God about it in prayer.

. . . .

RESPONDING TO HIS WORD

Day 38

WHEN LIFE HURTS

We were under great pressure . . . in our hearts we felt the sentence of death. But this happened that we might not rely on ourselves but on God, who raises the dead. He has delivered us from such a deadly peril, and he will deliver us. On him we have set our hope that he will continue to deliver us, as you help us by your prayers. Then many will give thanks on our behalf for the gracious favor granted us in answer to the prayers of many. –2 Corinthians 1:8b-11

. . . .

I don't know about you, but I am not fond of suffering. I'm the woman who told the doctor *before* labor that I wanted drugs and planned out which kind to take. I hate pain. And yet . . . it's unavoidable in this life, isn't it?

Paul has wise words for us when everything in life hurts. Even though he was one of Christianity's greatest missionaries, followed God closely, and loved Him deeply, he suffered. In these verses Paul recalls times when he was under such great pressure he wasn't sure he would be able to survive. Loving and following God did not guarantee a life of ease. In reflecting on these verses . . .

I need to remember that we, too, are not exempt from hard times. Trials don't necessarily mean we are out of God's will. Suffering can be a part of His very good will for us in light of His eternal plans.

I need to remember that our God is the Deliverer. We are weak and can't rely on ourselves. Our wisest course of action is to rely on God. Truly rely. He is able to deliver us. He has in the past, and He continues to rescue His people to this day. When a crisis comes, we can turn to the God who raises the dead. Seriously. Ponder that for a second. What a powerful thought! God is able to raise people from the dead. No trouble that comes, no trial, no problem, no stress could ever be too hard for His deliverance. Period.

I need to remember to pray. Paul knew that God works through prayer. He points out that the prayers of many resulted in the gracious favor God had granted him. Our prayers matter. They truly do. When we pray alone or together with other believers, God moves in a way that doesn't happen without prayer. Can I explain that? No, because I believe God is Sovereign as well. What He plans will come to pass. Somehow, though, He uses our prayers. We cannot neglect the important work of prayer.

I need to remember that answers to prayers increase our faith. If everything just went along swimmingly without issue or hindrance, we would assume that was the norm. We wouldn't look to God. However, when trials that seem insurmountable come—and the Deliverer shows up, we remember. We remember how desperately we need Him. We remember His power and our own weakness without Him. Like Paul, we give thanks for the gracious favor granted us in answer to the prayers of many, and our faith in Him grows.

Heavenly Father, help me to remember. Forgive me when I grumble and take offense at trials, as if somehow I should always have life as I want it. You, dear God, have larger and better plans. Help me trust You in the midst of trials. Give me strength and perseverance to pray, Lord. Show me the situations that need fervent prayer, and equip me to do the hard work of prayer for those in need. Thank You, Father, that You are the Deliverer. I look forward to my final deliverance one day right into Your holy Presence. In Jesus' Name, Amen.

GOING DEEPER
For those days when you have more time to ponder

Read 2 Corinthians 1:1-11.

Write out what you learn from Paul in this passage about the way God comforts us.

What do you learn from these verses about Paul's perspective on suffering?

Pick a favorite from these 11 verses. Write it out, and then pray, responding to God and what He is revealing to you through this verse.

. . . .

RESPONDING TO HIS WORD

Day 39

BUILD EACH OTHER UP

Encourage one another and build each other up. —1 Thessalonians 5:11a

• • • • • • • • • • • • • • • •

When we were first married, I managed to confuse Ray . . . a lot. Every time he turned around, I was waiting for him to praise me. "Look at this clean bathroom!" I'd announce with pride. He'd look puzzled at me and at the bathroom and just move on. In his world, you simply did your job. No one applauded when he showed up for work on time. No one noted that his shoes were shined every day. He did his job and hoped for a good review once a year.

His wife, on the other hand, seemed to want to be noticed at every turn. Ray used to joke, "I suppose you need me to admire the way you brush your teeth, too?" We "blame" this on my wonderful mother, who has encouraged and built up each of her children since they were born. (She actually did, by the way, point out to me once that I had done a great job brushing my teeth! Which made me brush all the better.)

To this day, my mom notices her children's accomplishments and delights in our achievements and gifts. She always, always points us back to God and how He is the One who gives us any abilities we have. The confidence we have in God and His work in us traces its roots to her encouragement. Part of the reason I'm a generally happy person today is because I had a mother who noticed me and built me up. I know full well that to feel treasured as a child is a gift indeed.

To *encourage* is to instill courage into another person. To build others up is to notice what is good and lovely about them—and to let them know. When we emphasize the virtuous and noble and wholesome traits we see in others, a desire grows in them to continue living up to those values. In fact, as followers of Christ, we are *called* to encourage and build each other up in Him.

As we go about our day, let's be on the watch for ways to encourage one another. One friend may be experiencing a difficult time and need extra courage

just to keep going, to keep praying, to keep believing. A quiet person at work or in the neighborhood is often overlooked. Watch for gentle ways to uplift that quiet one. Discover what words or actions will inspire and strengthen each person with whom you interact. Be especially aware of those closest to you. It's easy to take their actions for granted. Let's encourage our husbands and our children, our parents and our friends when we see the good they are doing. Let's build them up in a world that too often only tears them down. This is what we are called to do, according to Paul in his letter to the Thessalonians.

What about poor Ray and his wife's unrealistic expectations? Well, a wonderful thing has happened after years of marriage and "learning" each other. I have settled down and no longer feel quite the same need to have every completed task applauded. Ray, on the other hand, has grown more and more verbal, often letting me know how precious I am to him. It's worked out very nicely indeed.

Father, help me to notice the good in others. Show me who needs encouragement today. Help me to give them courage. Give me insight to know the best way to build others up in the faith. Thank You for every person who has given this kindness to me. Lord, help me to be one of the reasons someone feels happy today. And help me, just like my mom, to always, always point them back to You, the Giver of every good gift. In Jesus' Name, Amen.

GOING DEEPER
For those days when you have more time to ponder

Take a look today at Barnabas, a mighty encourager in the early church.

Read Acts 4:32-37.

We are introduced to Barnabas, called by the disciples "son of encouragement." How did he encourage and build up the believers?

Read Acts 9:26-27. Barnabas exercised courage in speaking up for Paul. Is there anyone you should speak up for, even though it might be unpopular?

Read Acts 11:19-26. In what ways do these verses show Barnabas as an encourager? List a few practical ways you can follow his example and be an encouragement in your home or school or workplace.

. . . .

RESPONDING TO HIS WORD

Day 40

IT'S DONE!

As far as the east is from the west, so far has he removed our transgressions from us. —Psalm 103:12

. . . .

I marvel at the wonderful forgiveness of our God, and I grieve for those who struggle to believe that He has truly forgiven them. There was a time in my life when I was one of them. I had not genuinely believed that I was forgiven.

When my girls were little, I tried so hard to be a good mom—but I made my share of mistakes. One was pushing my girls to look good on the outside so that I, their mother, would look good. One of my daughters, now grown, told me that as a child, she felt the burden of always acting right so that I wouldn't be embarrassed. It was not an easy yoke for her to bear and possibly encouraged her perfectionistic ways.

When I realized that my motivation for our daughters' goodness had often been external recognition rather than a desire for their inner souls to be right with God, I was heartsick. I apologized to them and cried out to God for forgiveness. The girls forgave me, and God forgave me.

However, I continued to bring it up. I told one daughter, especially, over and over, again and again, how sorry I was that she had felt such an impossible strain. One day, she took my hand and held it in her own and said, "Mom. Shhh! It's done. You are forgiven. Stop." I realized that I had still been beating myself up for something that had been forgiven. Psalm 103:12 tells me that my sins are removed. Gone. *It's done.*

Dearest one, once you have confessed a sin and asked forgiveness, you can rest in knowing that *It. Is. Done.* You are forgiven. Believe it. Don't stay trapped in self-condemnation. If you do, you won't be able to move forward with God's great plans for you. You'll be bound up in useless regrets. Take God at His Word when He says, "If we confess our sins, he is faithful and just and will forgive us our

sins and purify us from all unrighteousness" (1 John 1:9). He *will* forgive. He will *cleanse* you from *all* unrighteousness. I see no exceptions in this verse. You can believe it. You can bank on it.

Maybe you're thinking, she doesn't know my sins. She doesn't know my past, the pain I've inflicted, the evil I fell into, the shameful things I've done. For you, I would like to lovingly repeat: I see no exceptions in this verse. God doesn't categorize big and little sins. He freely, freely forgives all sin. Remember Peter's forgiveness after denying Jesus? Remember Paul's forgiveness for murder and acts of terror against Christians? And both men were mightily used by God. These sinners were entrusted with writing Scripture!

Take a moment and praise God for His wonderful, awesome, complete, and total forgiveness. We are given fresh, clean starts *every* time we ask. "As far as the east is from the west, so far has he removed our transgressions from us" (Psalm 103:12). Believe it. Receive it. It's done.

Dear Father, forgive me for not believing that You forgive me. Who am I to think my sin is greater than Your love or forgiveness? Forgive me for staying "stuck" in this place of regret and woe, instead of taking Your good hand and moving on to what You have planned to do through me. Give me faith, Lord, to trust You and to move on to fulfill Your good purpose for my life. Thank You, Lord, for total forgiveness. I am amazed and grateful. In Jesus' my Savior's Name, Amen.

. . . .

GOING DEEPER
For those days when you have more time to ponder

Read 1 John 1.

How does John express his absolute certainty about Christ, the Word?

Write out the verses that remind us that all of us sin. Why do you think John emphasizes this?

Does the memory of a past sin still entangle you? A sin that the enemy is using to keep you down and living in shame instead of victory? Get rid of it. Ask God to help you picture your sins being removed as far as the east is from the west. Declare out loud: "Thank You, God. It's *done* because of Your work on the cross." Whenever the enemy of your soul reminds you of this sin, thank God for the freedom of His forgiveness—and smile.

RESPONDING TO HIS WORD

Day 41

NEW THINGS

"Forget the former things; do not dwell on the past. See, I am doing a new thing! Now it springs up; do you not perceive it? I am making a way in the desert and streams in the wasteland." —Isaiah 43:18-19

I remember back when our youngest daughter was soon to marry. After her final trip home as a college student before her summer wedding, I wrote in my journal, "I have to confess that I've had some rough days. When Mary loaded up her car for college and headed out, she was truly not coming back except for visits. She's engaged to a wonderful, Christian man, the man I have prayed for. He loves the Lord, and he loves my Mary. It's an exciting and joy-filled time in our lives, but it's also a signal that I'm entering a new season. That stuff in her car will never return to New Hampshire, but will find a new home in Virginia."

I did spend a few days grieving, but then I began to look ahead for the "new thing." You see, as long as we have breath, when one season ends, another begins. One of the great joys of our lives as Christians is that we are a part of something so much bigger than ourselves.

How are you doing today? Are you facing a new season? Are you putting a child on the school bus for the first time? Is a move to a new location in your future? Have you just hugged your college freshman goodbye and cried all the way back home? Are you facing a frightening change? A health challenge you didn't ask for? Dear sister, take comfort with me that even though a season we loved is over, we have a God who delights in doing new things.

Whatever your season, we are members of the body of Christ, and we have literally been *assigned* work to do. Paul says, in Ephesians 2:10, "For we are God's handiwork, created in Christ Jesus to do good works, which God prepared in advance for us to do."

Scripture assures us that He makes a way even in the desert and brings streams to wastelands. He has a plan and a purpose for us as long as we live. I worked for a nonprofit ministry for over 20 years and loved it. Then, God called me to a season of caregiving. This led to the founding of Sweet Selah Ministries that allowed me a more flexible schedule and enabled me to write this devotional you now hold in your hands—a task I could do from home as I tended to Dad Gamble.

One day, I will likely enter another season. Perhaps on my own; perhaps in a wheelchair, limited in movement and ability; perhaps God will call me to a deeper work of prayer during the elderly season of my life. Life will always bring new things up to and including a new body in the new heaven and new earth. Praise God for that!

If you are in a season of change or loss, grieving is part of the process. As I waved goodbye to my youngest child, my heart was heavy, knowing that her first loyalties would now belong to the fine man she was marrying. God, in His Goodness, brought me through that season and enabled me to look forward to the next one. When we seek Him, He shows us what new thing He has for us. I love that we have been created for a purpose and that God has plans for each of us all the days of our lives.

Father, please bless the reader of this devotion today. Show her Your plans for this season in her life. Reveal to her Your purposes for the time and place in which she finds herself. Lord, give all of us eyes to see the new thing springing up. You are able to take a wasteland, a time of loss, and make it flow again with living water. Thank You! Bless and guide us as we look to You. Help us to fulfill Your good plans and purposes for our lives. In Jesus' Name, Amen.

· · · · · · · · · · · · · ·

GOING DEEPER
For those days when you have more time to ponder

Read Romans 12:1-8.

How do you practically live out the command to offer your body as a living sacrifice?

Paul challenges us to evaluate ourselves based on the measure of faith God has given each one of us. Why do you think that is the standard of measurement?

Read through the listing of some of the gifts of the Spirit in Romans 12:6-8. What gifts has God given you and how are you using them in this season of your life?

. . . .

RESPONDING TO HIS WORD

Day 42

JUST AS HE HAD DONE BEFORE

Now when Daniel learned that the decree had been published, he went home to his upstairs room where the windows opened toward Jerusalem. Three times a day he got down on his knees and prayed, giving thanks to his God, just as he had done before. —Daniel 6:10

• • • • • • • • • • • • • • • • •

The story of Daniel and the lions' den really begins with this verse. In order to trap Daniel, enemies in the royal court had convinced the king to create an edict that for thirty days no one in the kingdom could pray to any god except the king. This decree carried deadly consequences for the disobedient. They would be thrown into a den of very hungry lions. What a gruesome, horrific way to die! The decree and its punishment pretty much insured that everyone would obey, whether they wanted to or not—or, at the very least, make sure no one saw them praying to any other god.

I love this verse that records Daniel's response to the decree; nothing in his daily routine changes. Daniel's habit is to pray three times a day, and he prays in a prominent place in full view of a window. Faced with a huge crisis and a dreadful penalty, he prays *just as he had done before*. Seriously? It's hard to imagine this kind of incredible bravery. He didn't even sneak a prayer. He just did what he always did. He prayed to the living God he loved. It's almost as if Daniel didn't notice the edict. His course was set on honoring God and that was what he was going to do.

As I'm sure you have, I've experienced times of unsettling crisis in my own life. In those times, it's hard to think straight. If you're an emotional creature like I am, your mind races in circles and even regular duties and chores are hard. It seems, however, that somehow the normal day-to-day duties still manage to get done, like on autopilot. That's the way it's been for me with my quiet times—

a daily habit now for over 30 years. It's what I do in the morning. I wake up, make a cup of tea, settle into my favorite corner of the couch, and meet with God. When a crisis comes, the habit is ingrained. That's what I do even when life seems to be whirling around me.

When times are tough, it's wise to continue the good spiritual habits we've formed. We go to church. We attend our Bible study. We meet with God daily. Just as we had done before. That continuity stabilizes us. It grounds us. These spiritual disciplines declare to a watching world—and to the unseen world—that we go to God always. We go when it's sunny and happy, and we go in the midst of the storms. That's what we do.

Dear one, the next time a crisis comes—and, sadly, in this world we will have trouble—keep doing the right thing. Even when your emotions are in disarray. Even when you are fearful. Even when it's unpopular. God miraculously delivered Daniel from the lions, but come what may, be a Daniel—even if you have to enter a lion's den. God will be there with you.

Father, I'm grateful for this time of relative peace in the United States where I live. I know full well, Lord, that all could change in a moment. Help me come to You no matter what, "just as always" until You take me Home. I love You, Lord. Help me to show it by the way I live. In Jesus' Mighty saving Name, Amen.

· · · · · · · · · · · · · · · · · ·

GOING DEEPER
For those days when you have more time to ponder

Read Daniel 6.

How did Daniel's character land him in trouble with the bad guys?

In this story, the king was bound by his own laws and quite frustrated. Why?

How did Daniel's obedience to God influence a king? How does this challenge you in your own sphere of influence?

Ask God to show you any changes you need to make in order to be an influence for good in your culture.

. . . .

RESPONDING TO HIS WORD

Day 43

YOKED

Come to me, all you who are weary and burdened, and I will give you rest. Take my yoke upon you and learn from me, for I am gentle and humble in heart, and you will find rest for your souls. For my yoke is easy and my burden is light. —Matthew 11:28-30

• • • • • • • • • • • • • • • • •

I've been pondering what it looks like to be "yoked with Christ." Have you checked out a yoke lately? It's a bit intimidating. Looks rigid and confining. Once one ox is yoked to another, they're basically stuck together until someone unyokes them. Sounds . . . restrictive, doesn't it? So, why would Jesus want us yoked with Him? Why would He use the analogy of a yoke when we are weary and burdened?

Being yoked means being close. All day long. There's no "feeling stuck" when you're linked with the One who loves you most. It's a joy to be close. It's a dream come true.

Being yoked means we aren't doing life alone. In fact, just as the stronger ox bears the weight of the yoke when training an inexperienced ox, Jesus bears the weight for us. That's why His yoke is easy.

Being yoked with the Lord means we have direction. I can spin in circles on my own, never sure what to do next. If I'm bonded with Him, I have a path, a plan, a purpose.

I want to be united like that with the Lord Jesus. At least . . . I do when my heart is right. I'm ashamed to say there are days when I refuse the yoke. I'm not sure I want to go where He will lead me. And yet, He knows me intimately. He knows the future. *He loves me.* Why in the world would I want to go anywhere but where He leads? So . . . how do I obey the command to "take my yoke upon you and learn from me?"

Y - Yield. I need to be willing to yield my will to His, trusting that He knows better than I do what the day will hold and how I can best fill it with work that matters. He knows best the work or service He will guide me into when we are yoked together.

O - Obey. I need to obey—if He says, "go left," I go left, even if I had favored the right. Practically, that means I'm willing to give up my plans even when they are interrupted—maybe by someone in need or a whisper from the Spirit to stop and make a call. It definitely means I must walk in obedience to the commands in His Word.

K - Know. I need to know Him so well that I trust Him as the leader in our yoke. He is truly gentle and humble in heart, and I really will find rest for my soul. Often, He calls me to stop and be still, something I would seldom do on my own. My God is good, and His plans for me are good. The more I know who God is, the more I can trust Him.

E - Expect. I need to walk in expectation when I take His yoke. He has a plan to guide me. My job is simply to stay attached. Close to Him. Remembering He is right there with me. A day yoked with Him is a day of adventure and accomplishment. It's a day of victory, because I'm walking the path He has marked out for me, doing work that matters for His kingdom.

Picture yourself today in Jesus' wonderful yoke of comfort, closeness, and guidance.

Dear Lord, thank You for this invitation to willingly take Your yoke upon me all day long. I choose to do that today. I want to be that close to You. Help me to seek Your guidance and Your will at every turn. Remind me to turn to You in prayer when I'm perplexed or angry—or happy. Help me consult You and remember You in every circumstance of the day. Lord, forgive me for the times I wander in circles because I'm not yoked. Today, Lord, I willingly yield to Your directions and to Your good plans. Today, Lord, I take Your yoke upon me. In Jesus' Name, Amen.

GOING DEEPER
For those days when you have more time to ponder

Read John 14.

List some of the ways the Holy Spirit helps us stay yoked to Christ.

What words of encouragement does Jesus give His disciples about life after He returns to Heaven?

What verse reassures you as you seek to take His yoke upon you?

• • • • • • • • • • • • • • • •

RESPONDING TO HIS WORD

Day 44

THE TANGLED NECKLACE

You have searched me, LORD, and you know me. You know when I sit and when I rise; you perceive my thoughts from afar. . . . Such knowledge is too wonderful for me, too lofty for me to attain. —Psalm 139:1-2, 6

Back when she was five, one of our girls was broken-hearted over a necklace that had become hopelessly tangled. It was a thin, gold-plated chain and had somehow knotted up so that I despaired of ever untangling it. In fact, I suggested we give up and buy a new one. "No!" she exclaimed. Through her tears she let me know how special it was to her. We couldn't throw it away!

We were at her grandparent's home at the time, and Ray's father, one of the most patient men I have ever known, said, "Give it to me." Painstakingly, over the course of several days, he worked on that little inexpensive chain with tweezers and time and concentration. Little by little, he worked out each and every knot. When he presented an unraveled chain like new to our daughter, she was delighted. He was, too, as he gently placed it once again around her neck.

I've been wrestling with some pretty huge dilemmas. Several families dear to me are in crisis, and when I hear their stories, I feel overwhelmed by the sheer complexity of the problems. So many layers of hurt, mistrust, and confusion. Answers completely escape me. As I was praying, God brought to my mind the memory of that tangled chain. Yes, that's how I can pray for big and sticky problems.

I imagine myself as a little girl with a tangled necklace. I don't have a clue how to unravel the mess, but I know the One who does. I hand that tangled trouble to God through prayer. He knows when we sit and when we rise; He knows our thoughts from afar; and He is quite able to untangle it all. I'm not sure why I think I have to make suggestions to God in my prayers about how to solve problems!

He is quite able to unscramble the worst of messes with wisdom and patience. All He asks is that we bring them to Him.

As you pray for problems great and small, remember that God is wise enough to resolve and straighten out the most knotted jumbles. We never need to give up in despair. One day when we reach Heaven, perhaps He will reveal to us some of the tangles that were beautifully straightened out because we asked in faith-believing prayer for His help. Never stop bringing the messes and the muddles and the "impossibilities" to Him.

Father in Heaven, how thankful I am that You care about our problems. You are able to help in the hardest of situations. Help me trust You and remember to bring every tangle to You. Give me patience as I pray and wait for Your answers. Lord, I want Your will, Your way, in Your time. In Jesus' Name, Amen.

. . . .

GOING DEEPER
For those days when you have more time to ponder

Read the following passages on God's wisdom: Psalm 104:24; Proverbs 3:19-20; Daniel 2:19-22; Romans 11:33-36.

What do you learn about God's wisdom from these verses?

Which verse resonates most strongly with you and why?

List a few of the tangled messes you are currently experiencing—either in your own life or in the lives of your loved ones. Hold them up to the One who can untangle and ask for His help.

. . . .

RESPONDING TO HIS WORD

Day 45

THOUGHTS ON TOAST AND TRAGEDIES

And the God of all grace, who called you to his eternal glory in Christ, after you have suffered a little while, will himself restore you, and make you strong, firm and steadfast. —1 Peter 5:10

• • • • • • • • • • • • • • • • • • • •

It always feels wrong to me. While others are hurting, I'm doing mundane things like making toast or taking the dog for a walk. The dissonance is jarring. Today, my mind is spinning from the latest horror in the news of mass destruction and the endless disasters that preceded it: hurricanes, earthquakes, large and growing refugee camps, boats capsizing with frantic refugees on board, and children terrorized by evil men. Endless stories of suffering on a scale I have never experienced and can barely comprehend.

Then, there are the "smaller" stories in cancer wards and nursing homes, on city streets, and in broken homes that break my heart as well. I feel bewildered at the juxtaposition of suffering elsewhere and life as usual right where I am. Should I be making toast today—and planning a party, of all things? Is that even right?

And yet . . . perhaps carrying on is the best response in a world gone mad. After the tears have come, the prayers have been prayed, the money has been sent, perhaps the best we can do is to simply go on living, grateful for a pocket of quiet in our corner of the world—and more aware than ever of life's fragility. To live consumed by fear and terror solves nothing. Maybe a heightened sense of gratitude is a good thing. Maybe a desire to hold our loved ones a little closer is heaven-sent. So, I'll be grateful today for the undeserved quiet I've been given in which to make my toast. I'll give thanks and hug my loved ones close. And I'll pray. Will you pray with me?

Dear Heavenly Father, hold and comfort all who are hurting today. Be tender with them. Show them mercy and glimmers of light in the darkness. Remind them that You are Light and that our stories do not end with death, but rather truly begin . . . that eternity is reality and life after death is seriously even more important than life now because it goes on forever.

Show me ways to help. Give me a generous heart. Prompt me to pray and to show kindness wherever I can. Help me to appreciate and value the mundane days of making toast as a rare gift on this broken planet. And, if and when my time of suffering comes, oh, Lord, make me ready. Help me to always feel my hand in Yours, holding me close and drawing me ever nearer to my forever life with You.

Lord Jesus, we await Your return, longing for the day when all will be made right. Until then, guide us and show us how to live grateful lives in light of Your sacrificial death on our behalf. Always, Lord God, we look to You. In the Name of Jesus, help us. Amen.

. . . .

GOING DEEPER
For those days when you have more time to ponder

Read 1 Peter 4:12-5:11.

Peter offers dear words of encouragement in this letter. Choose a verse that is particularly encouraging to you and write it out.

Write a prayer responding to God for His encouragement in the verse you chose.

I have no idea what the latest tragedy in the world will be at the time you are reading this devotion, but you know. Stop and pray.

RESPONDING TO HIS WORD

Day 46

TREASURING WORDS

And they were holding golden bowls full of incense, which are the prayers of God's people. —Revelation 5:8b

· · · · · · · · · · · · · · ·

Some moms make beautiful scrapbooks to remember their children's growing up years. Others save favorite clothes, T-shirts, special blankets, or toys. I collected words—my children's crazy toddler words. Carefully recorded in baby books, there are almost as many funny sayings as pictures. I loved listening to them as they learned to form words.

Mary, as a toddler, was a hungry girl. Long prayers before dinner were not for her. Her very first prayer at the supper table was direct and to the point: "Food. Amen." Kathryn's first prayer was similar: "Thank oo pears." She neglected the traditional Amen. Still under two years old, Kathryn said to me one day, "Shh . . . the people in my ears are sleeping." I'm still trying to figure that one out, but she was quite serious about the need for quiet.

When Kathryn had an elevated temperature, she would place my hand on her forehead and say, "Feel my fever." Mary was afraid of "alibators," and they both asked for "calcium" when they wanted milk because I had told them milk contained calcium. A ramp was a "tramp," and Mary was very sorry one day that she had "avregated" me. We ate "pasghetti" and "hangubbers" at mealtimes, and every day yielded fresh treasures. Oh, what fun to hear our teeny ones' mixed-up attempts!

I loved every precious, muddled expression that came out of their mouths. Their words weren't eloquent. Some were confused. Sometimes they made very little sense. Yet, because these were my dear girls, their words and expressions were my delight and my joy.

Revelation 5:8 tells me that God, too, values His children's words. Our prayers are somehow saved in golden bowls. Seriously. Our stumbling, confused prayers are of great value to our Heavenly Father. Why? Because we are His delight and joy, and we are trying to communicate with Him. We're His kids. What we say matters to Him. Never feel that your prayers are not of high enough quality. Just come to your Lord, who has given you permission to call Him *Abba*—a term of endearment for Dad, like Papa. Share with Him in your halting, stumbling way, the desires of your heart. He hears you. He treasures time spent with you, His precious child.

Father, how thankful I am that You call me child. Not superhero. Not famous speaker. Just a kid. Yours. Oh, Lord, thank You for welcoming my stumbling, fumbling words when I cry out to You in pain and confusion. Thank You for Your Spirit within me, interpreting those words and even speaking for me when I can't (Romans 8:26). You hear my broken cries. I thank You in Jesus' Name, Amen.

· · · · · · · · · · · · · ·

GOING DEEPER
For those days when you have more time to ponder

Read Romans 8:1-27.

Romans 8:1 declares there is no condemnation for those who are in Christ Jesus. Reading the verses that follow, why is this so?

Find every reference to prayer and the Holy Spirit in this section. What do you learn about each and the link between the two?

Think about your own prayer life. Are you free to simply pour your heart out to God? Does it help to know you can just be like a child?

Pray. Speak freely to Him now about whatever is on your heart.

RESPONDING TO HIS WORD

Day 47

NEVER GIVE UP

Then Jesus told his disciples a parable to show them that they should always pray and not give up. —Luke 18:1

• • • • • • • • • • • • • • • •

My sixth grade Sunday school teacher was a 65-year-old man named Rocky Taylor. Despite the obvious gap in age between Rocky and us sixth graders, we loved that guy. He was our favorite. He delighted in teaching us about the Lord Jesus and made the Bible come alive through skits and talks. His zeal for the Lord shone so brightly, we were all changed. I'll never forget Rocky or his influence in my life.

The really cool thing about Rocky Taylor, though, was his wife Esther. She had married Rocky in her early twenties. As a follower of Christ, Esther knew that Scripture warned against being "unequally yoked," but she ignored that and married Rocky, an unbeliever. She knew she was being disobedient, but at the time she didn't care. Shortly thereafter, when Rocky and she were in the midst of a very "rocky" marriage . . . she cared very much.

However, Esther was a woman of prayer even in the midst of her unhappiness. She never gave up on Rocky, and she prayed every day for his salvation. For forty years. Yes. She prayed and prayed. She longed for her husband to know Jesus. And one sweet day, Rocky Taylor, forty years after his wedding, fell headlong in love with the Savior of his soul.

I had the joy of being one of the many beneficiaries of Esther's persistent, prayerful, faithful wait for her husband to know her Lord. Once Rocky turned his life over to the Lord, there was no stopping him. He was going to make up for lost time in his fervor for his Savior and King!

Perhaps, like Esther, you are waiting for a loved one to accept Christ or return to Him. Don't stop praying. Don't give up. Persevere like Esther did. God's timing is not ours, but He hears every prayer. Encourage others who are waiting, hoping, longing to never lose hope but keep asking the Savior to rescue their loved one.

Father, give me a faithful heart, ready to pray for those who still need to find You. Help me to wait with patient trust. And give me a zeal like Rocky's to share the good news of Your Son! In Jesus' Name, Amen.

· · · · · · · · · · · · · · · ·

GOING DEEPER

For those days when you have more time to ponder

Read Luke 11:5-8 and Luke 18:1-8.

Both of these parables have an element of audacity. What is quite bold and brazen in each case?

Jesus links audacity to persistent prayer. Why?

What request have you been praying for many long years? Pray again, right now, with the audacity to believe the God of Heaven hears you and will answer according to His good will.

· · · · · · · · · · · · · · · ·

RESPONDING TO HIS WORD

Day 48

CHEERING OTHERS ON

May the LORD answer you when you are in distress. . . . May he send you help. . . . May he give you the desire of your heart and make all your plans succeed. May we shout for joy over your victory and lift up our banners in the name of our God. May the LORD grant all your requests. —Psalm 20:1a, 2a, 4–5

A sad, but true, fact: It's often hard to be happy for others when they surpass us. Someone else gets that promotion at work when I'm struggling to make ends meet. Someone else's child makes the varsity team, and my child's sitting on the bench. Someone else has a child, and I'm left wondering why I don't. Someone else has a happy marriage, and I'm bitterly struggling in mine. The list is endless. Someone is always surpassing us at something, and in today's world of social media, we know about it right away. The celebration is quite public.

Even though we know we should rejoice in others' good news, the evil sins of comparison and envy often choke out our kindness. How easy it is to fall into the pit of self-pity. I know, because I've been there—and that pit is a bad place to be.

I have found that one of the best antidotes for the sins of comparison and envy is . . . prayer. When we pray for another's promotion or child or well-being, we share in it. Their success becomes "ours," and we want God's best for them. How much easier it is to rejoice in victories when we have played a small part by asking for them! Today's scripture, Psalm 20, is loaded with good wishes for the victories of others. What a great example for us to practice—freely giving our good wishes and rejoicing over the achievements of others.

The choice to rejoice—instead of comparing—leads to peace and joy and the good pleasure of God Himself—and that's a very good place to be.

I'm filled with gratitude for each one of you who are reading this book.

I have prayed for you, that God will bless you mightily as you study His Word through these pages. I join with the psalmist today and pray for you . . .

"May the LORD answer you when you are in distress. May he send you help. May he give you the desire of your heart and make all your plans succeed. May we shout for joy over your victory and lift up our banners in the name of our God. May the LORD grant all your requests" (Psalm 20:1a, 2a, 4–5). *In Jesus' Name, Amen.*

. . . .

GOING DEEPER
For those days when you have more time to ponder

Read Psalm 20.

List all the "prayer wishes" mentioned in this psalm.

Reread verse 7. We don't tend to trust in horses and chariots nowadays, but what do we tend to trust more than God Himself?

Is there someone in your life who has enjoyed success in an area you feel you lack or have failed? Stop and pray for them right now. Ask God to bless them abundantly and to take away any feelings of envy or comparison that would rob you of joy.

. . . .

RESPONDING TO HIS WORD

Day 49

PRESCRIPTION FOR RENEWED STRENGTH

We're changing things up today: A gift from God's own words to you, a gift of renewed strength for the weary. I pray that His Word will reassure you today of His power and His deep love for you.

Here's what to do. Quietly take a deep breath and whisper, "Teach me, Lord." Then, read the scripture below out loud. Marvel as you speak it. Ponder each word. Rejoice that you serve a glorious God. Please read out loud, savoring each precious line. Don't just skip over any word.

Read it once again. And perhaps even one more time, dear one. My prayer is that the One who calls each star by name will renew your strength today as you meditate on His unfailing love.

Lift your eyes and look to the heavens:

Who created all these?

He who brings out the starry host one by one,

and calls them each by name.

Because of his great power and mighty strength,

not one of them is missing.

Why do you complain, Jacob?

Why do you say, Israel,

"My way is hidden from the LORD;

my cause is disregarded by my God"?

Do you not know?

Have you not heard?
The LORD is the everlasting God,
the Creator of the ends of the earth.
He will not grow tired or weary,
and his understanding no one can fathom.
He gives strength to the weary
and increases the power of the weak.
Even youths grow tired and weary,
and young men stumble and fall;
but those who hope in the LORD
will renew their strength.
They will soar on wings like eagles;
they will run and not grow weary,
they will walk and not be faint.
—Isaiah 40:26–31

Father, speak to us as we meditate on Your Word. Thank You, in Jesus' Name, Amen.

• • • • • • • • • • • • • •

GOING DEEPER
For those days when you have more time to ponder

Read Isaiah 40.

What do you learn about God from this chapter?

Of all the verses, which speaks to you most today? Write it out.

Write down a prayer, thanking God for His Word and for that special verse.

· · · · · · · · · · · · · · · ·

RESPONDING TO HIS WORD

Day 50

LIVING WATER

Jesus answered her, "If you knew the gift of God and who it is that asks you for a drink, you would have asked him and he would have given you living water." —John 4:10

• • • • • • • • • • • • • • • •

Our daughter experienced a frightening season of debilitating headaches when she was in high school. When one hit, she'd have to leave class and lie down in the nurse's office, sometimes for hours.

We tried remedy after remedy all without success. Finally, in desperation, we were referred to a headache specialist who recommended a very strong medicine to combat the headaches. This particular medication was normally used to stabilize epilepsy patients! Instead of helping, she hated the way this medicine made her feel—even more than she hated those headaches.

The whole time she was going through this ordeal, I would ask her, "Are you drinking plenty of water?" That irritated her no end. "Yes!" she would reply. As it turned out, the anti-seizure medication ended up bringing the whole issue to a head (no pun intended!). How she hated that medicine. So, I asked if she would be willing to chart her water drinking for one week. Guess what? She forced herself to drink eight 8-ounce glasses of water every day, and her headaches totally disappeared.

When she made a record, she could see in black and white that she had been sipping water all day but had not been drinking any significant amount. The answer to her problem was simple. Her body was screaming for more water. Once she truly hydrated herself, she was just fine.

You know, we can sometimes be a "sipper of water" in our spiritual lives. We go to church, and we pray occasionally. We sip. Think about it, if we never stop to really drink and hydrate from the Living Water, we won't have the strength we

need for our days of activity and service. We need to take in time with Jesus on a daily—even hourly—basis. Just as my daughter needed to drink water, we need to truly drink in the Word of God and spend significant time in prayer with Him to be spiritually hydrated. When we come to Him, hearing His Word, crying out to Him from our hearts, *He satisfies*. May God bless you with His Living Water as you spend time with Him drinking deeply.

Father, show me ways to drink, not sip. Help me to study Your Word and to ponder. Remind me to come to You with troubles, big and small, and sit at Your feet. I thank You that You truly satisfy my thirsty soul. Help me to long for You as a deer pants for water (Psalm 42:1). In Jesus' Name, Amen.

. . . .

GOING DEEPER
For those days when you have more time to ponder

Read Psalm 42.

Hear the longing for God in the psalmist's cry. Name a time when that longing was strong in you.

How does the psalmist cope with his "downcast spirit"? How can you cope using some of his methods?

List ways you plan to drink fully of the Living Water this coming week.

. . . .

RESPONDING TO HIS WORD

Day 51

ABBA

For you did not receive a spirit that makes you a slave again to fear, but you received the Spirit of sonship. And by him we cry, "Abba, Father." —Romans 8:15

I sat me down and had a good, long cry. I had informed my husband as he left for work that day my plan was to cry my eyes out. He didn't comprehend this in the slightest and looked quite relieved that I didn't seem to think him necessary to the process. After he left, I pulled our overstuffed chair up to the fire, put on sweet worship music, grabbed a box of Kleenex, and simply sobbed. It was just what I needed.

It was a time when trouble seemed all around me in the lives of dear ones—cancer, wayward children, broken marriages—and, oh, how I hurt when those close to me are hurting. The sadness builds up in me until I know it needs to come out in tears. So I sit and I cry . . . to the One who listens and understands best. My Abba.

What a wonder that the God who created the world with His voice, the God who is Holy and who lives in unapproachable light, is also called Abba. The term *Abba* is one of endearment for a daddy, like saying "Papa." Closeness, intimacy, and deepest love are the meanings wrapped up in the name Abba.

Paul assures me in the verse above, that I did not receive a spirit that makes me a slave again to fear. I don't have to let fear overwhelm me. Instead, the Holy Spirit dwells in me, and, when I am grieved or wounded or just plain sad, I'm free to run to the One who calms my fears and steadies me.

Some earthly fathers are available and affectionate, but being human, sinful, and limited in time and energy, no father is always available like our Abba. To Him, we can come at any time, sure of a warm welcome, a heart of love, and a compassion that is greater than any we have ever known.

My time with the Lord that morning left me feeling relieved . . . refreshed . . . ironically, even cheered. Crying out my hurts and disappointments to God brings perspective and comfort.

Are you feeling burdened today by the cares of this world? The trials you are facing? The pain of those dear to you? Remember you have a God who calls to you, "Come to Me." You have a God who loves you and longs for an intimate relationship with you. You have an *Abba*.

Dear Father, thank You for the great privilege of allowing us to call You Abba. Thank You for Your gift of closeness to us in our times of greatest need—and in our times of joy. Oh, Abba, keep this child of Yours close to You always. In Jesus' Name, Amen.

· · · · · · · · · · · · · ·

GOING DEEPER
For those days when you have more time to ponder

Read Galatians 3:26 – 4:7.

What does God say through Paul in this passage about your right to call God, *Abba*?

Reflect on your own earthly father. If his example made it easy for you to believe God could be "Abba," then thank God. If your earthly dad's example lacked in some ways—or many ways—whisper your forgiveness and spend a few minutes thanking God for being the perfect Father.

Read Galatians 4:4 again. Ponder the phrase, "When the set time had fully come, God sent . . ." What does "fully come" mean? What does this teach you about God?

· · · · · · · · · · · · · ·

RESPONDING TO HIS WORD

Day 52

SEARCH ME

Search me, God, and know my heart; test me and know my anxious thoughts. See if there is any offensive way in me, and lead me in the way everlasting. —Psalm 139:23–24

· · · · · · · · · · · · · · · · · ·

When our daughters were little, each one used to come to me terribly aggrieved at the sin of the other one. They were pretty much experts at seeing their sister's failings and were often quite helpful in their suggestions for parental discipline! It reached the point that when an argument surfaced, I sent *both* girls to their rooms and asked them to reflect—not on what their sister had done, but on what *they* had done. What was *their* part of the quarrel? I would then ask each one to share with me her own wrongdoings, instead of accusing her sister.

Don't we grown-ups easily find ourselves doing the same thing? We notice others' faults, while excusing our own. Like when I'm irritated with my husband for playing solitaire on his computer when I thought he was grading papers. And yet . . . don't I often scroll Facebook when I need a break from writing? Why is it "not okay" for him to take a break, when I do the same myself? Good grief. Sometimes we can be so quick to excuse ourselves and so self-righteous toward others.

All of us can learn a lesson from David's prayer in Psalm 139. Instead of faultfinding, what about asking God to search our own hearts? Knowing that God is good, loving, merciful, and ever ready to forgive, we can ask Him without fear to show us our faults. He *wants* to forgive and wash us clean once again. How refreshing it is to be forgiven and have a fresh start! How thankful I am that we worship a God of grace. Still . . . I'm thankful that He has standards and asks me to recognize sin as sin. Only when I'm aware of my own sinfulness can I understand how desperately I need a Savior. And . . . once I'm aware of my own sinfulness, I'm less likely to point the finger at someone else.

Pray with me today.

Search me, O God, and know my heart; test me and know my anxious thoughts. See if there is any offensive way in me, and lead me in the way everlasting. Thank You, Lord, for Your sweet forgiveness and enduring love. In Jesus' Name, Amen.

. . . .

GOING DEEPER

For those days when you have more time to ponder

Read Psalm 139.

List the various ways God "knows" you.

Is there anyone in your life whose sin has aggrieved you to the point that it is affecting the way you live? Ask God to help you forgive. Turn to Him with the dilemma. Remember that forgiveness of another presumes they have sinned. It does not excuse sin or overlook it.

Sit before the Lord and read Psalm 139 out loud. When you reach verses 23-24, stop. Wait to hear what God would have you confess. Gladly confess and be *free.* God *always* forgives. Completely.

. . . .

RESPONDING TO HIS WORD

Day 53

HEART MUSIC

Speak to one another with psalms, hymns and spiritual songs. Sing and make music in your heart to the Lord, always giving thanks to God the Father for everything, in the name of our Lord Jesus Christ. —Ephesians 5:19-20

When our daughter Kathryn was in kindergarten, her three-year-old sister Mary and I walked her to school down a pretty little path in the woods. Toddler Mary would valiantly keep up with her big sister on the way to school, and I was free to follow behind carrying lunchbox and backpack. Inevitably, she would tire on the way home, and I ended up carrying her.

On our walk back, Mary would "sing" to me. I can still hear her tiny voice making up songs about birds and butterflies and trees and flowers and about the good God who made them. The songs didn't rhyme and had no recognizable tune. They welled up out of a happy child's heart—and they made this mother's heart overflow with joy. I absolutely loved listening as my little girl sang out of the fullness of her heart to the God she already adored.

Mary didn't need to sound profound or even beautiful in the way the world would define it. She just had to be herself, expressing her little heart with joy to her mom and her God. In the same way, I don't have to make my prayers sound impressive to please God. No grandiose or profoundly wrought sentence structures needed. I can simply warble a prayer song of thanks to Him from my heart. And, because I am His child, it brings Him joy.

As you go about your daily duties today, join me in singing a little song of thanks to the One who loves us so. We truly have much to be thankful for. May God be pleased to raise up a huge and glorious choir of folks who love Him and sing His praises!

I'm filled with gratitude when I think of you . . . faithfully meeting with the Lord through the pages of this devotional book. My wish for you today is that you may have music in your heart.

Lord, how grateful I am that You love me. Thank You for Your created world full of delightful beauty. Give me the eyes of a child to see the beauty in a butterfly or a cloud high in the sky. Help me to sing, Lord! I want to make music in my heart for You, my Father and King. In Jesus' Name, Amen.

GOING DEEPER
For those days when you have more time to ponder

Read Psalm 8.

What inspires this psalmist to marvel?

Write your own short psalm of praise to God.

Where do you go to enjoy God's creation? If you aren't regularly out of doors in some capacity, is this a habit you might want to cultivate?

RESPONDING TO HIS WORD

Day 54

GOD'S OWN HANDIWORK

For we are God's handiwork, created in Christ Jesus to do good works, which God prepared in advance for us to do. —Ephesians 2:10

. . . .

I've been busy crocheting. Each time we're expecting a new grandchild, that little one receives a blanket from their Nina (me!) in colors the parents choose. Everywhere I go—to doctor's offices and volleyball games and meetings—the blanket goes with me. It's important to me that I finish in time for that little one to be covered with it right away at birth. I pray for this unborn child as I crochet and spend many happy hours imagining him or her wrapped up in it.

Check out the verse above. Don't you love that word "handiwork"? It makes me think of women making quilts and men carving fancy chairs. Creating handiwork requires a willingness to invest a great deal of time and energy personalizing a project and making it unique. When it comes to Nina blankets, no two are alike. Each one has its own colors and patterns. (Each one also has its own carefully hidden mistakes—I'm far from perfect.)

God, who is perfect, has crafted us. That is what He does. We read in Psalm 139 that even before we were born, He created our inmost being. He knit us together in our mothers' wombs. We are fearfully and wonderfully made. Even those parts of us we might consider "mistakes" were allowed by Him for His good purposes. All of us have our own unique personalities and quirks. Each one of us was made with a very special purpose. Each one of us has specifically planned work that God has assigned to us. Wow. God has planned our paths ahead of time, and all we have to do is stay close to Him, allow Him to lead us, and allow Him to produce fruit in our lives.

You and I are God's own handiwork created in Christ Jesus to do those good works God had planned for you even before the beginning of time. Amazing.

Father, help us to fulfill Your purposes for our lives. Show us Your paths prepared ahead of time and enable us to walk in them with joy. In Jesus' Name, Amen.

. . . .

GOING DEEPER
For those days when you have more time to ponder

Read 1 Corinthians 12.

What do you learn about the value of spiritual gifts? How do various gifts fit together? How should spiritual gifts work in the church body?

List every gift you find mentioned in this chapter. Put a check mark by the ones you believe God has given you. (By the way, it's not vain to acknowledge that you have gifts. The word *gift* implies that you did nothing to merit it. Spiritual gifts are given to you by God that you might use them to bless others.) If you aren't sure about your gifts, talk to other Christians and ask them what they see in you. Or, ponder what you do that serves God and brings you joy.

What kind of path are you on right now? Is it wide, easy, and sunny or full of ugly twists and turns that frighten you? After answering this question, ask God how He wants to fulfill His good purposes in you on this part of your life journey. He will tell you.

. . . .

RESPONDING TO HIS WORD

Day 55

GETTING UP AGAIN...AND AGAIN

For though a righteous man falls seven times,
he rises again. —Proverbs 24:16a

. . . .

Our first kitten was a doozy. Her name was Tiger Lily—"Lily" was added to let folks know she was a girl, but "Tiger" was her descriptive name. Her antics kept us wavering from laughter to consternation. Early in her career as a jumper, Tiger Lily repeatedly tried and failed to leap high enough to reach the top of our dining room hutch. It was an elusive goal that tormented her—and *us* as we watched her attempts and failures! She would size it up, then crouch and spring. She would hit the side of the hutch with a frightening force and fall to the ground over and over. We tried to warn her. We tried to stop her. We cringed. We marveled as she shook herself off from a fall and immediately launched, airborne, to try and fail again. What kind of crazy cat was this? They really *do* have nine lives. We felt like hers were getting used up all in one day.

Within a couple of days, though, Tiger Lily had mastered that jump and was queen of the hutch. Despite the thunks, the failures, our dire warnings, predictions, and interventions, she had tried and tried, again and again—and she did it! She enjoyed her reign on top of that hutch, her favorite perch, for many a year. Now *that's* persistence.

In the Bible, we find a real live human example of getting up again. And again. The remarkable story of Joseph and his repeated setbacks is found in Genesis 37-50. I encourage you to take the time and read the full story, but briefly, Joseph was hated by his brothers who sold him into slavery in Egypt. He worked his way to the top as head over all his master's possessions until he was falsely accused of rape—and imprisoned. Once again, he worked his way to the top and was put in charge of all the prisoners. At one point, Joseph had a chance at freedom, but, instead, another crushing disappointment. He was betrayed, forgotten,

and languished in prison another two years. Setback after setback. Joseph spent the best part of his young adulthood rising only to fall again.

Why didn't he give up? What was his secret? He never stopped being Joseph, servant of the Most High God. No matter what was thrown at him, he kept getting up and doing the right thing. Day after wearisome day, year after tiresome year. He served faithfully when things went well and when things went sour. He just did the right thing. And then at long last, in God's good purpose and timing, Joseph was miraculously put in charge of all Egypt.

I want to be persistent and faithful like Joseph. Sometimes I, too, feel like my life is a series of setbacks. Everything seems to be going well, and then a crisis hits . . . again. I know I'm not alone. This is actually the human story. All of us face difficulties all of our lives. The times of relative calm are wonderful, but they don't last. Jesus clearly told us that "in this world you will have trouble," and we can pretty much expect it. The question is: what are we going to do with our latest trouble?

Proverbs 24:16 teaches us that the righteous man gets back up. Over and over again. Why? I believe it's because the "righteous man" is the one who knows that he is only righteous because of Christ. Once we know we belong to Christ, we know how our story ends. We know that no hard thing in our life will ever be wasted or come without purpose. We know that God uses all things to shape us into the person we were meant to be if we simply submit to the lessons within the trials. We know that God does, indeed, work all things together for great good for those who love Him. We never have a reason to despair. A happy ending does await us, even if it's not fully realized until we see Jesus face to face.

That's what keeps us getting back up. The purpose of it all. The promise that someday all will make sense. We'll see how even the hard things were used in God's plan for ultimate good. Let's never stop being the ones God called us to be—servants of the Most High God. Like Joseph, let's keep serving and trusting day in and day out and leave the end results in the hands of the One who has a purpose for us in it all. Don't ever stop getting back up.

Lord, forgive me when I want to sink into the pit when bad things happen. Help me to look for Your strong hand that is always available to haul me out and set my feet on the Rock once again. Father, I trust You.

I trust that all You allow has purpose even if I can't see it. I trust that the "getting back up" is what shows You my faith and what enables me to point others to You. Your plans are good. I thank You that the troubles I face, I don't face alone. You are always with me—and that makes my story a happy one! How I praise You in the name of Jesus who saves. Amen.

. . . .

GOING DEEPER

For those days when you have more time to ponder

Read Genesis 40:20-23 and Genesis 41:1-40.

How do we know from these verses that Joseph had continued to walk with God despite being forgotten in prison—even after the chief cupbearer had promised to try and secure his release?

Have you experienced a time in your life when things just kept going wrong, even though you were trying to do right? Write down your memories of that time, how it felt, and how you reacted.

Joseph shows great humility when he shares with Pharaoh what God has revealed. What are some practical ways you can point to God when complimented or consulted?

. . . .

RESPONDING TO HIS WORD

Day 56

AVREGATING

But God demonstrates his own love for us in this:
While we were still sinners, Christ died for us. —Romans 5:8

• • • • • • • • • • • • • • • • • •

One time when my children were preschoolers, I was having a very bad day. All these years later, I cannot even remember what on earth had put me in such a foul mood. I do remember that I was in one. I was stomping about and muttering in a most ungodly fashion when three-year-old Mary wandered into the room. Her little eyes grew big and wide, and I realized I had frightened her. "Mary," I said, "Do you know why Mommy is so upset?"

She calmly and sadly took her thumb out of her mouth and answered, "Because I am *avregating* you." Oh no! My heart sank. My stomping about had absolutely nothing to do with my precious girl, and yet here she was taking the blame.

I was humbled by this incident, and it worked change in me that I have never forgotten. I had failed to communicate to Mary the deep love I have for her, and, typical of children, she had assumed she was somehow at fault for my behavior. My bad mood evaporated as I hugged her and held her, assuring her of my love.

Oh, how thankful I am for God, my parent, who is never in a bad mood. He reassures me over and over and over again that I am deeply loved. The Bible is packed with verses that express His boundless love for us. He knows we need the reassurance every bit as much as Mary did that day.

One of the most meaningful verses to me says that "God demonstrates his own love for us in this: While we were still sinners, Christ died for us" (Romans 5:8). God showed His love by dying—for us—and we were unworthy sinners. I pray that God continues to tell you, dear one, that you are loved and cherished and that—even when you are "avregating"—He is still faithful in that love.

Father, You knew we'd need to be reassured that You love us. Thank You for the reminder that You died for us before we ever even turned to You. Thank You for a love so deep and wide and high and true. In Jesus' Name, Amen.

GOING DEEPER

For those days when you have more time to ponder

Read the following verses and soak in God's love for you. When you finish reading, write a letter to Him expressing what His love means in your life, how it makes you feel, and how it changes you.

Nehemiah 9:17	Isaiah 43:1-3	John 3:16	Ephesians 2:4-5
Psalm 86:15	Jeremiah 31:3	John 15:12	Ephesians 3:16-19
Psalm 136:26	Zephaniah 3:17	Romans 8:37-39	1 John 3:1

RESPONDING TO HIS WORD

Day 57

FACE TO FACE

I have much to write to you, but I do not want to use paper and ink. Instead, I hope to visit you and talk with you face to face, so that our joy may be complete. —2 John v. 12

I keep a pretty tidy house, but you'd never know it to look at my refrigerator, which is plastered with pictures. Scattered amongst the photos on my fridge, you'd also see precious, handmade drawings from grandchildren that are simply amazing (of course no bias here!). You could spend hours perusing the collection on that refrigerator. You see, I love faces.

Human faces are truly remarkable. Each one is distinct. Even identical twins are a smidge different from each other. Our Creator God delights in variety and expresses it in the way He makes us. Thoughts and attitudes that can be hidden in texts or emails cannot be as easily hidden when we are face to face. I think that's why John, in writing to his friends, states that he didn't want to use pen and ink. He wanted to be with them, face to face.

I've pondered this little verse, and I identify with John. We live in a world with ever-increasing means of communication. However, like John, I don't think anything beats actually being together and seeing the expressions in each other's eyes. No online church service can ever really take the place of worshiping next to a Real Live Person with a face you can read and love. When we are physically present with each other, it's a lot harder to hide—unless we are phenomenally talented at deception. What we are thinking shines out through our eyes, our smiles, our mannerisms. Face to face is vulnerable. Face to face is real. Face to face is good.

John writes that he hopes to visit and talk to his friends face to face, "so that our joy may be complete." Yes. When I see my dear grandchildren who live far

away, when my daughters and their husbands visit, when I spend time with my parents, my joy is complete. I love being physically with them.

Social media and communication through technology can be a huge blessing. It's a great way to stay connected with family and friends, far and near. However, I urge you (and me) to carefully guard against spending too many hours of precious life in a virtual world. We can make ourselves look "pretty" on social media and avoid hard topics. That's dangerous. Let's live real, actually taking time to be physically *with* others, setting aside the distractions of devices and being truly face to face, getting to know them—the good and the bad together. Spending time with another human being is a gift and a joy, even if it's also an effort.

Heavenly Father, thank You for the variety of faces in my life. Help me to make time to be physically present with the people You've placed in my life—in church, in my neighborhood, and in my home. Thank You, Lord, that You know my face well. You knit me together in my mama's womb (Psalm 139:13) and You have counted the hairs on my head (Luke 12:7). Thank You that there will come a day when I will have the incredible, awesome privilege of seeing You, face to face (1 Corinthians 13:12). Longing for that day, Jesus! I pray in Your Great Name, Amen.

GOING DEEPER
For those days when you have more time to ponder

Read Acts 28:17-31.

List the face-to-face times in this portion of Scripture.

What lessons can you draw from these times that apply to the way you live today?

Ask the Lord to show you who needs your face this week, and find a time to be there for them.

RESPONDING TO HIS WORD

Day 58

CHANGES

Every good and perfect gift is from above, coming down from the Father of the heavenly lights, who does not change like shifting shadows. —James 1:17

I recall a Mother's Day back when our daughters were preschoolers. They had decided to surprise me with breakfast in bed! I guess they thought it a bit of a tradition since I had delivered each of them breakfast in bed on their birthdays.

They had no problem finding the cereal. However, instead of milk, they chose a carton of heavy cream I'd purchased for a recipe I was planning to try. The bowl was first filled with said cream. Then, realizing there wasn't much room left for cereal, they sprinkled a few bits on top. They added a glass of juice, a napkin, and a spoon; placed it all on our special breakfast-in-bed tray; and carefully carried it up the stairs. Well, they tried to be careful. Later, I found a trail of cream and orange juice giving away each bump on their long pilgrimage up to my bedroom. Oh, the look on their faces! They were so proud and insisted on staying to watch me enjoy my creamy breakfast. Yikes!

It's hard to believe those two little girls are now mothers themselves. Where did the time fly? Wasn't it just a few short years ago they were wearing braces and taking piano lessons? How could their high school graduations have occurred more than a decade ago? How could their own tiny firstborn boys now be walking and talking and going to school? I feel an incredibly weird juxtaposition of emotions as I cheer on each new step . . . and look back with a tad bit of wistfulness on all that has gone before. Change happens. That's life.

I praise God that one blessed part of life does *not* change. James declares that our God does not change. He's not like shifting shadows. In a world that is uncertain and erratic and unpredictable, He is the same yesterday, today, and

tomorrow. God's love does not change. God's faithfulness does not change. His offer of salvation does not change. His Word does not change. How grateful I am that in the midst of life changes, our God stands as a Rock.

Father, thank You that You are my place of safety and assurance. Thank You that You are always . . . You. Help me, when I face changes, to remember that You knew all about them before they even happened. You know the beginning from the end, and You are with me through it all. I am ever grateful for the solid assurance that You do not change. I love You, Lord. In Jesus' Name, Amen.

· · · · · · · · · · · · · · · ·

GOING DEEPER
For those days when you have more time to ponder

Read the following passages that all point to the immutability of God (a God who does not change): Psalm 102:25-27; Malachi 3:6; Hebrews 1:12; Hebrews 13:8; Revelation 1:8.

Which passage resonates most with you and why?

What is comforting to you about an immutable (unchanging and unchangeable) God?

What changes are currently happening in your life? Pray for His grace and strength to receive them as from His hand, trusting in Him no matter what.

· · · · · · · · · · · · · · · ·

RESPONDING TO HIS WORD

Day 59

GENEROUS

"For the kingdom of heaven is like a landowner who went out early in the morning to hire workers for his vineyard." —Matthew 20:1

• • • • • • • • • • • • • • • •

Have you ever prayed and prayed and then *prayed* for someone to know Christ as Savior . . . for decades? I have. I plead with God to open his eyes to the truth. I share the gospel with him. And I wait and hope that he will see the beauty of the kingdom of heaven before he dies, bowing his head to the King. I will be sad if it takes all his life to find Christ, but I want to believe that it's never too late . . . even in the last minute of life.

That's why I love the parable Jesus tells of the workers in the vineyard as recorded by his disciple Matthew (Matthew 20:1-16). On first read, the story seems absurd and totally unfair. The owner of the vineyard hires workers throughout the day, but ends up paying the same wage to each one at day's end. Yes, you read that correctly. Each one gets the exact same amount, whether he worked all day or a half day or was hired near quitting time. *What?* In Jesus' parable, the workers who toiled all day in the hot sun were understandably irritated that their wages weren't higher than those who hired in last. I have to admit I wasn't too thrilled about this either when I read this parable long ago. But now? Why, it's one of my favorites.

I want all my dear ones who do not yet know Christ to come to Him, to know Him, to be saved by Him. Their time on earth is getting shorter and shorter, and my heart hurts. How I long for them to receive the free gift of eternal life before they die—even if it's on their deathbeds. I want them to understand there really is a Kingdom of Heaven awaiting those who answer God's call. I want that kind of grace given to them, even if they never do a single "good deed" for Him in their entire lives. Because I love them.

That's why I love Jesus' vineyard tale of generosity and grace. The owner chastises the grumbling workers who labored all day. "Take your pay and go. I want to give the one who was hired last the same as I gave to you. Don't I have the right to do what I want with my own money? Or are you envious because I am generous?" (Matthew 20:14-15). Hear this. *God wants to be generous.* He has the right to give eternal life to those who have served Him faithfully all their lives and to those who discover in their last hours that they've missed the most important Truth of all. We are not saved because we do great and marvelous things for God. We are saved because He chooses to save us. Because we say yes to His invitation to come to Him. We do the good-deed stuff out of our love for Him. We serve Him because it's our joy. And if He chooses to call a dear one to Himself at the very end of life? Praise His Name for His Mercy!

I am clinging to this story in hope for *my* dear one. I am so grateful I serve a generous God.

Heavenly Father, thank You for Your story of generosity and kindness. Thank You that You are not willing that any should perish, but that all should come to repentance (2 Peter 3:8-10). Oh, Lord, You see the ones we are praying for today. Draw them to Yourself. Show them the reality of heaven. Continue to open their eyes to the truth of the unseen life with You. Father, how I praise You for Your patience with us, receiving those who, like the thief on the cross (Luke 23:39-43), are slow in coming to know You. I am in awe of Your great and gracious generosity. I thank You in Jesus' Name, Amen.

GOING DEEPER
For those days when you have more time to ponder

Read 2 Peter 3.

What do you learn about salvation from this chapter?

What do you learn about the end of the world and the beginning of heaven from this chapter?

What verse strikes you most forcefully? Write it out. Then write a response to the Lord based on that verse.

Sweet Addendum: This day's devotion was written about my dear father-in-law, who lived with us before he died. Rejoice with me! Nine days before his death, he received Jesus Christ as his Lord and Savior. God answered my prayers, and I have the assurance that I will see him again someday.

. . . .

RESPONDING TO HIS WORD

Day 60

A TIME TO WEEP

There is a time for everything, and a season
for every activity under the heavens:
a time to be born and a time to die,
a time to plant and a time to uproot, . . .
a time to tear down and a time to build,
a time to weep . . .
—Ecclesiastes 3:1-4a

. . . .

It was a time in my life when I had to deal with some crushing news. Inside, my heart was screaming in pain, but for some absurd reason, I thought I should act "all together" on the outside to be a "good witness" for Christ. I smiled. I assured people I was fine, that God was in control, that I trusted Him. I gave a stirring speech about His Goodness. I believed what I was saying—but inside I was dying. And that's because I wasn't crying. You know what? It's okay to cry.

Every time I read the story of Joseph, I admire this brave, young man who continued to do what was right even when circumstances continued to go very wrong. Guess what else Joseph got right? Crying. Weeping. Yes, he did. Read with me what happened when Joseph saw his younger brother again, alive, after years of separation. "Deeply moved at the sight of his brother, Joseph hurried out and looked for a place to weep. He went into his private room and wept there" (Genesis 43:30). Later, when Joseph sees his beloved father, he weeps again. "Joseph had his chariot made ready and went to Goshen to meet his father Israel. As soon as Joseph appeared before him, he threw his arms around his father and wept for a long time" (Genesis 46:29).

These passages are a comfort. Joseph reassured his brothers that those actions they had meant for harm (selling him into slavery), God had meant for good.

Still . . . this same Joseph . . . wept. He wept a very long time. I suspect he was weeping for the lost years, weeping for joy at a longing finally fulfilled. Even though God had worked miracles for great good throughout Joseph's life . . . it was *hard*.

When I face a difficult season or devastating circumstances, even though I know my God is Sovereign and has a plan in the midst of the pain, it's okay for me to cry about that pain part. In fact, it's healthy.

Dear one, when you face a season of sadness or trauma, remember that there is a time to cry. Let your tears out in sweet release or in emotional torrent. Pretending happiness is not the answer. Tears not shed fester in a body. When we cry, we are being truthful. Sometimes life hurts. When it does, it's a time to cry, and tears are our Creator's gift to us, helping us release the pain inside.

King David wrote, "You [God] keep track of all my sorrows. You have collected all my tears in your bottle. You have recorded each one in your book" (Psalm 56:8 NLT). Take comfort that God knows when you cry. He cares enough to keep a record! Someday, "He will wipe every tear from [your] eyes, and there will be no more death or sorrow or crying or pain" (Revelation 21:4a NLT). Until then, it's okay—and even good—to cry.

Heavenly Father, how I thank You for these sweet promises that one day You will wipe our tears away, and that You even make a record when we cry. Oh, Lord, You notice. You care. Help me to be honest with what I feel, taking time to weep when needed, remembering that I don't have to pretend to be strong. Thank You that I can simply come as Your little child and cry when I need to, and You, the God of all comfort, will be there for me. In Jesus' Name, Amen.

· · · · · · · · · · · · · · · ·

GOING DEEPER
For those days when you have more time to ponder

Read Genesis 50.

How many times does this chapter mention that Joseph wept?

How did Joseph respond to his brothers' fears that he would take revenge once their father had died?

Do you have a hard time seeing God's good in a specific situation that was unfair or wrong? Write out a prayer asking the Lord for His help in seeing the situation through His eyes.

· · · · · · · · · · · · · · · · · ·

RESPONDING TO HIS WORD

Day 61

CHOOSING FELLOWSHIP

They devoted themselves to the apostles' teaching and to the fellowship, to the breaking of bread and to prayer. Everyone was filled with awe. . . . They broke bread in their homes and ate together with glad and sincere hearts, praising God and enjoying the favor of all the people. And the Lord added to their number daily those who were being saved. —Acts 2:42–43a, 46b–47

Ray and I have attended a whole lot of churches during our married life. During his 17 years of military service, we moved 14 times, including seven moves to different states or countries. I soon learned that I could never replicate the same church we had just left, any more than I could find the exact same friend in my new location. At first, this was a source of distress to me. I yearned for the church I had left behind, remembering how comfortable I'd felt and how many friends I'd gained there.

Eventually, I learned to let go of expecting and hoping that my experiences would be the same in each place we settled. Instead, I began to celebrate the uniqueness of the particular body of Christ where God had placed us this time. I soon discovered that wonderful fellowship can happen in very diverse groups of people when we all honor the Lord and His Word. Each church in its turn became my favorite as I focused on all we had in common. Ray shakes his head at our very long Christmas card list, but how could I trim it? Each church in each place has yielded treasured friendships. Our involvement in every one of them brought us such joy!

God never meant for us to do life alone. Something beautiful happens when a body of believers is devoted to the Word of God (the apostles' teaching), to fellowship, to the breaking of bread, and to prayer. In fact, this list from the book of Acts is a great guide for choosing a local church:

Is your church devoted to the apostle's teaching ... God's Word? Make sure your church takes seriously the Bible's claim that it is God-breathed. People who value the Word have a standard and a guide for life—and for doing life together.

Is your church truly a fellowship? Do people love each other and want to be together sharing each other's burdens?

Are you breaking bread with members of your church? Are you in each other's homes, getting to know one another in all the nitty gritty reality of life? Are you enjoying fellowship with glad and sincere hearts?

Are you also breaking bread in the sense of taking Communion together? Remembering Christ's death until He comes? Is Jesus central in your church?

Is your church a place of prayer? When you have a burden, are others ready and willing to genuinely pray for you? Are you faithful to pray for the pastors and teachers at your church?

Are you adding to your number? Is your church a place where individuals are coming to salvation in Christ? Is your church active in reaching out to the lost and hurting through service to the community and the world? Does your church extend a warm welcome to those who are seeking?

Of course, this is the ideal, and no church filled with sinners, as all churches are, will do everything perfectly. However, your local body of believers should be actively working toward these goals. Let's lead the way in how we live and interact with church members. I want to be devoted to the local church, living out God's commands in the context of Christian fellowship and family. How about you?

Heavenly Father, show me, please, how to help my church follow this example in Acts. Give me a genuine love and concern for the people in my church body. Help me to be faithful in prayer and in hospitality, entering into the lives of those who worship with me on Sunday morning. Oh, Lord, may our church be a place where it can be truly said, "And the Lord added to their number daily those who were being saved!" In Jesus' Name, Amen.

GOING DEEPER
For those days when you have more time to ponder

Read Acts 2.

Note that the believers were "all together in one place" when the Holy Spirit came. What does this teach about meeting together?

Study Peter's message at Pentecost. How does he use the Scripture to teach? What part of his sermon resonates most with you?

Walk through Acts 2:42-47, asking the Lord to help you become this kind of church member.

. . . .

RESPONDING TO HIS WORD

Day 62

HANGING ON

For I am the LORD your God who takes hold of your right hand and says to you, Do not fear; I will help you. —Isaiah 41:13

. . . .

Hidden away at the very back of our Christmas tree hangs an elf, his little hand clinging to a tree branch. He's a scruffy fellow made of pipe cleaners and felt, and he's not in tip-top condition, poor guy, grimy with age and discolored by countless hands touching him over the years. You see, I made him myself . . . in kindergarten.

I know. I know. Why on earth is this guy still hanging around? My mother admired my little work of art way back when and faithfully displayed him every year. In fact, our family Christmas tree was filled with kids' Sunday school projects and school artwork my mother treasured. When I married, I brought my pipe cleaner man along with me, since he had grown into a bit of a tradition. I couldn't quite imagine a tree without his one-armed-hang on a branch somewhere, and he has graced each Christmas tree in our home since.

I will say that he has become a family joke of sorts. My children and husband roll their eyes at his unsightliness. "Hide him in the back!" they demand. I protest, declaring he should be front and center and merriment ensues. That elf has brought a lot of crazy laughter to our tree decorating. See? He belongs on the tree just for amusement's sake.

At times in my life I feel a lot like that little elf. I'm not in tip-top condition, a bit wobbly—but I know my job, and I will do it with all my remaining strength. I'll cling faithfully, not to a tree branch, but to my Heavenly Father's hand.

"I, the LORD, have called you in righteousness; I will take hold of your hand" (Isaiah 42:6a).

At a time of deep distress in my life, God, as He so often does, directed me to this verse. In context, these words are spoken to the Messiah Jesus, but at that moment in my life, the Lord whispered to my heart, *Cling to Me, and I will take hold of your hand.*

Faithfully cling to the Father's hand, dear one. There is no better place to be . . . especially when you feel a bit undone like my little Christmas elf.

Heavenly Father, how I thank You for the picture You give in Scripture of Your big hand reaching down and gripping mine. Help me, Lord, to cling. I don't want to wander off and leave Your side. Keep me close and comfort me when I'm feeling undone. Thank You that Your love for me never depends on my appearance or abilities. You loved me before I even knew You. Take hold of my hand, dear Lord, and never let me stray. In Jesus' Name, Amen.

- - - - - - - - - - - - -

GOING DEEPER
For those days when you have more time to ponder

Read Revelation 3.

This chapter contains letters to churches that were pretty bedraggled. How does God encourage them to keep going?

What are the dangers these churches are warned about? Which one do you personally relate to most?

Are you feeling wobbly? Pray, and ask God for His big hand to hold yours. Do you know someone else who is feeling wobbly? Pray for them as well.

- - - - - - - - - - - - -

RESPONDING TO HIS WORD

Day 63

IT'S THE LITTLE THINGS

And if anyone gives even a cup of cold water to one of these little ones who is my disciple, truly I tell you, that person will certainly not lose their reward. —Matthew 10:42

Once upon a time, when our girls were ages four and two, Ray and I saved our money to buy them the Deluxe Fisher Price Kitchen for Christmas. That kitchen had everything . . . stove, fridge, pots, pans, sink. Wow. I was so jazzed for them! Opening it up on Christmas morning was such a thrill. I gleefully showed them all the features of this wonderful (expensive) present.

That night when I went upstairs to tuck them into their beds, I confidently asked, "So, girls, what was your very favorite Christmas gift this year?" Without skipping a beat, they bounced on their beds and shouted with glee, "the Chapstick!" . . . um, what was that? We spent a ton of money on a deluxe kitchen set and their favorite present was . . . the *Chapstick*? Well, then. *That* taught me several lessons about gift giving.

Sometimes, it's the little things that mean the most. I think they loved that Chapstick because it seemed grown up to them, like Mom and Dad. They already played about in my real kitchen, so the fake one was okay, but not as appealing. The wonderful Fisher Price Deluxe Kitchen Set was given away a few years later still looking remarkably new. The Chapstick? They used up those tubes and asked for more. Chapstick was fun. Chapstick was "grown up." After that, little tubes made an appearance every year in their stockings.

Do you sometimes feel small and inadequate in a world of *Big Needs*? I do. All around me are big opportunities . . . to feed the poor, the homeless, serve orphans, take in a foster child. The needs around me are overwhelming, and my own resources of time and money so tiny. I'm tempted to do nothing, because I can't do a great deal—and that's the wrong perspective.

God notices the tiniest act of kindness, even a cup of cold water given in His Name. Like my girls delighted in those teeny tubes of Chapstick, little things—helpfulness, sympathy, compassion, gentleness—are like cold water to a thirsty soul and can yield great joy. Yes, let's do big things in Jesus' Name when we can, but all of us can choose to make it a way of life to watch for the little things—needs we *can* meet that brighten lives.

Heavenly Father, thank You for this reminder that even a cup of cold water given to one of Your tiny ones is seen by You and rewarded. Help me to notice ways I can serve others and help me to do so with joy. Show them to me, Lord, as I go about my day today. Use me, Your little one, for good in Your kingdom work. In Jesus' Name, Amen.

· · · · · · · · · · · · · · · ·

GOING DEEPER
For those days when you have more time to ponder

Read 2 Kings 4:1-7.

What big problem did this widow have, and what resources did she possess to meet the crisis?

How did Elisha help her take the little she had to meet her great need?

List some "little" resources you have to serve the King (time? money? talents?). Next to each item on your list, write how you are using this resource, or how you could use it in service to the Lord.

· · · · · · · · · · · · · · · ·

RESPONDING TO HIS WORD

Day 64

EVEN THE HAIRS ON YOUR HEAD

Indeed, the very hairs of your head are all numbered. —Luke 12:7a

• • • • • • • • • • • • • • • •

Some days, when I was a new mother, it took me an entire hour to change a diaper. I actually did know how to change one fairly quickly. What slowed me down were the coos, the smiles, and the earnest conversations my baby was attempting with me. I had no idea what she was saying, but she delighted in my attention. And, as she burbled, I simply loved watching her every move and expression. My agenda for the day came to a halt. I was enthralled with that precious, little baby.

Today, I'm grandmother to an ever-growing number of dearly loved grandchildren. And I'm back to the one-hour diaper change whenever I have the chance. If one of my grandbabies has something to "say" in their baby burbles . . . they have my full and delighted attention. I carefully study every picture our daughters send us, examining facial expressions and hairstyles and clothing. These are "mine," and I love them. Every single little detail about them is a marvel to this "Nina."

Hard to fathom, but true: the God of the Universe also stops, pays attention, and delights in you and me. He "quiets you with his love, he rejoices over you with singing" (Zephaniah 3:17b). This beautiful imagery reminds me of a parent leaning over a crib (or a changing table) and purely delighting in their child. In his gospel, Luke quotes Jesus stating an amazing fact—the Father cares about us so dearly that even the very hairs of your head are all numbered. Now *that* is focused, passionate love. I love my girls and grandchildren, but I've never even attempted to count the hairs on their heads. Jesus is making the point that we are precious beyond measure to the Father.

Do you believe this? Can you grasp this? How much He loves you? You are the beloved child of the best Father ever. And He can tell you exactly how many hairs are on that cherished head of yours.

Stop a moment and breathe that in. Right now. It's staggering.

Thank You, Father God. Thank You for the reassurances, over and over, that we are deeply loved. We don't deserve it. We don't understand it. But oh, how wonderful! It's true. You sing over us. You are that close. That involved. That loving. We love You, too, Father. Help us to love You more. In Jesus' Name, Amen.

GOING DEEPER
For those days when you have more time to ponder

Read Zephaniah 3.

List the many ways God's people have disappointed Him.

Write out His plan to save them. Find every encouraging thought and write it down.

Choose the verse that stirs you most. Write it out, and make it personal by placing your name in the verse as appropriate. Thank God for His love in your life.

RESPONDING TO HIS WORD

Day 65

DON'T DELAY...OBEY

I will hurry, without delay, to obey your commands. —Psalm 119:60 NLT

· · · · · · · · · · · · · · · · · ·

It was a cold and frosty day in March. Our family was living in Massachusetts, and we owned a long-legged beauty of a dog named Porsche. A Great Dane mix, Porsche was well named for she loved to run.

On this particular morning, we all needed to get out of the house and move our legs, so my two little girls and I took Porsche to a nearby park. As soon as we let our eager dog out of the car, she galloped directly toward a pond. Too late, I realized the pond still had a covering of ice. I started to panic. The ice would be thin at this time of year.

In vain, I shouted, "Porsche, come!" She paid no attention as she frolicked onto the pond, slipping and sliding and running full tilt ahead. Finally, she heard me screaming at the top of my lungs, but, when she began racing back toward shore, I watched in horror as the ice cracked beneath her, and she fell through. After a terrifying time, she managed to scramble, break up the ice, and half swim toward us. With strict instructions to the girls to stay on shore, off came my shoes, and I waded out staying only knee deep to try and help our desperate dog. With shaking hands, I was able to break up the ice in front of me, and Porsche managed to free herself and clamber toward me. Finally, she had a clear path back to shore. By then, both she and I were soaked, freezing cold, and trembling. Both little girls were crying.

If only our disobedient dog had come when I first called.

How often I'm like Porsche. Too busy to listen, I dash about wildly, not stopping to hear the voice of the One who loves me calling, *"Come to Me."* In my self-centered pursuit of my own will and pleasures, I don't listen to God's words, *"Follow Me (don't race ahead of Me.)"* The result is often sadly similar to Porsche on the ice. By not going to the Lord first and receiving my direction from Him,

I need rescuing from the messes I create. As the psalmist writes, "Hurry, without delay, to obey [His] commands." It's the only way to keep off thin ice.

Father, help me listen to Your voice, today. Remind me of Your good commands, as I go about my duties. I want so much to walk in obedience to You. Keep me off that thin ice, Lord. I choose solid ground with You. In Jesus' Name, Amen.

. . . .

GOING DEEPER
For those days when you have more time to ponder

Begin reading Psalm 119, noting verses that speak about obedience to God's Word. Stop when you've found 10 verses.

What are the central truths in these verses about obedience to the Word?

Are there any verses that particularly challenge you?

Are you consistent in your daily time with the Lord, coming to Him first?

. . . .

RESPONDING TO HIS WORD

Day 66

PUDDLE SITTING

Let us not become weary in doing good, for at the proper time we will reap a harvest if we do not give up. —Galatians 6:9

Sometimes, I'm a puddle sitter. I don't recommend it. A friend introduced me to this little word picture. Her illustration goes something like this: At times, on the path of life, we come across a gigantic puddle. We can't go around it, so we have to trudge through it. However . . . we do not have to sit down in defeat right in the middle of the puddle and splash ourselves all over with dirty water. Keep going, and eventually we will come to the end of that puddle.

Do you ever tire of slogging through a situation trying to be the one doing it right? Isn't it tempting to just stop struggling, sit, and wallow in gloom for a bit? The problem with puddle sitting is that we stop moving forward. We lose momentum. We're splattered with depression and heaviness. The longer we sit, the harder it is to stand back up. Paul calls this becoming weary in doing good. I think we've all felt that way at times.

Here are my biggest temptations to puddle sit:

Difficult People Problems. It's downright hard to be patient with some people, especially ones who seem to have no patience for us. It's challenging to continue treating folks kindly when their words seem deliberately calculated to hurt. Turning the other cheek, loving our enemies without seeing any change in them, is tough. It's wearisome.

Caregiving. Whether it's getting up in the night to care for a teeny infant or turn an elderly parent to prevent bedsores, giving, giving, giving can grow wearisome.

Praying for a situation that just gets worse. Have you ever prayed for healing, and the person you pray for doesn't improve, maybe even dies? Have you ever asked God to rescue a family in marital strife, only to watch them divorce?

Have you ever prayed for the return of a prodigal, who then sinks deeper into the mire? That's wearisome.

How easy it is to become discouraged and want to stop the good work we're doing! How *do* we keep going when we don't see results?

We remember that the very act of walking through that situation—through that messy puddle—is pleasing to our God and Father.

Whether the difficult person ever acknowledges your acts of kindness, God sees them. He will grow a harvest of blessing in your own soul as you practice love and reject bitterness. Each time you struggle out of bed in the middle of the night to serve a needy one, God sees you, and He will reward you. Ultimately, you are serving Him. When you pray and pray and don't see the answer you desire, the very act of continuing to pour out your heart to God reaps in you a harvest of closeness to Him. Lessons will be gleaned along the way, even if He never answers as you wish.

God gives us a sure promise in Galatians 6:9. We *will* reap a harvest if we do not give up doing good. Yes! When we come to a hard stretch in the road, let's keep on doing right, knowing He sees, and He is pleased. Let's find joy in walking straight through that puddle, honoring our God with every sloshy step. Hey. We might even find ourselves singing in the rain!

Father in Heaven, I want to do good. Help me, please, when I hit a weary stretch, to keep going, keep trusting, keep knowing that You go with me, and You do reward those who follow You. In Jesus' Name, Amen.

· · · · · · · · · · · · · · · · · ·

GOING DEEPER
For those days when you have more time to ponder

Read Acts 12:1-19.

What event do we read about in Acts 12:1-2 that might discourage believers from "doing good" and praying for Peter in prison?

Even though the faith of the believers was small, what was the eventual result of their prayers?

What situation in your life at the moment is tempting you to "puddle sit"? Pray, and ask God to give you strength to continue "doing good" and not grow weary or give up.

. . . .

RESPONDING TO HIS WORD

Day 67

LETTING GO

*I desire to do your will, O my God; your law
is within my heart.* —Psalm 40:8

. . . .

When our grandson was almost two, we gave him his very first Matchbox car. He loved it. However . . . he had no idea what to do with it. He held it in his chubby, little hands and admired its wheels. His daddy kept trying to persuade him to let go of the car, so he could show him how it could race across the kitchen floor, but our toddler would have none of it. He held on more tightly, refusing to release it and totally unaware of the enjoyment he would have if he would just let it go and learn from his dad. Oh, little boy . . . you are missing out on the best with your tight-fisted grip!

Watching him, I realized that, all too often, I do the same thing. I hold tightly onto my will, convinced that I know best—how a loved one should grow in Christ or how a certain situation should be resolved. My hand clutches my plans, and my wonderful, Heavenly Father gently, patiently, repeatedly pleads, *"Give your plans to Me. Let me show you how it works."* Oh, the release and joy that come when I relinquish my way and trust Him to do what is best.

Jesus modeled this desire to do the Father's will throughout His life on earth. In John 6:38, He declares, "I have come down from heaven not to do my will but to do the will of him who sent me." In Matthew 6:10, He teaches us to pray, "Your kingdom come, your will be done, on earth as it is in heaven." We read Jesus' plea in Luke 22:42, "Father, if you are willing, take this cup from me; yet not my will, but yours be done." Over and over, Jesus' life demonstrated His obedience to the Father's way, the Father's wishes, the Father's will.

Just as my little grandson learned to release his Matchbox car, when I release my tight grip on a situation and turn it over to God, He can move circumstances in directions I could not have imagined. God knows far better how to lead

and direct in the way we should go in any and every situation. Why do I think I know best, when the Maker of the very ones I want "fixed" stands ready to take over and work in them? He sees the beginning from the end.

Heavenly Father, help me to hold my hands open before You in surrender and submission to Your best, trusting You with those I love and with all my plans and hopes and dreams. In Jesus' Name, Amen.

GOING DEEPER
For those days when you have more time to ponder

Read Luke 22:39-71.

Did Jesus understand His Father's will and plan? Did Jesus like this plan and look forward to releasing His will to fulfill it?

What were the results of His obedience, yielding His will to the Father?

Ask God to help you give your plans over to Him, and whisper, "Thy will be done."

RESPONDING TO HIS WORD

Day 68

FAITHFUL

"But while he was still a long way off, his father saw him and was filled with compassion for him; he ran to his son, threw his arms around him and kissed him." —Luke 15:20b

. . . .

The story of the prodigal son always moves me. I was meditating on the verse above, and God inspired me to write this poem about His unfailing love. Join me today in marveling at His love.

FAITHFUL

You are Faithful.
We walk angrily away, taking our demanded inheritance with us
Leaving You who shared all You owned
To grieve
And watch for our return.
We waste our inheritance.
Our bodies are overfed and under exercised, creating disease and atrophy.
Our time is frittered away on things that don't matter
And don't satisfy.
Our money goes to foolishness while most of the world starves.
Our minds worry, fret, gossip, become embittered
When they could be enriched by Your Word and Your Spirit
You.

Yet You are Faithful.
You wait.
You watch.
You humble Yourself with longing for Your foolish prodigals.

And when we turn . . . You *run* to us.
Oh, incomprehensible *Love*—You run!
You embrace.
Your *Joy* pours out in party . . . fatted calf . . . best robe and ring
For the very ones
Who squandered what You gave.

Make me faithful.
Help me love and wait for those who squander
And trample their inheritance.
And when they turn
Give me incomprehensible *Love*
Unabashed *Joy!*
Just like You.

Make me faithful, Lord. Help me to love and wait for those who squander and trample their inheritance. Forgive me, when I do the same. Remind me, that if I turn, You are there. Help me, when a prodigal returns, to show incomprehensible love . . . unabashed joy . . . just like You do. In Jesus' Name, Amen.

GOING DEEPER
For those days when you have more time to ponder

Read Luke 15.

In the parables of the lost sheep and lost coin, the owner diligently seeks and searches for them. In the story of the prodigal, the father waits and yearns, but does not go after the son. What can we learn from this as we deal with lost ones in our own lives?

List the ways in this chapter that God shows His love for those of us who wander.

Pray for a prodigal, a wanderer—and take comfort in knowing how deeply God cares for them.

. . . .

RESPONDING TO HIS WORD

Day 69

TRUST

But those who trust in the LORD will find new strength. They will soar high on wings like eagles. They will run and not grow weary. They will walk and not faint. —Isaiah 40:31 NLT

- - - - - - - - - - - - - - - - -

Watching our two daughters learn to swim taught me a lesson about trust. One daughter listened to her instructor and boldly pushed off from the side of the pool. She was quite confident that if she failed her instructor would catch her and not let her drown. The other one clung to the side of the pool with terror in her eyes and refused to budge. Guess which one learned to swim first?

Oh, how often in my own life have I allowed fear to win out over trust. When I come to God with a burden, do I trust that He has taken it and is carrying it for me? When I do, the very process of laying my cares at His feet gives me new strength. I have confidence that I have brought my request, my anxiety, to the right place. I am strengthened in my soaring, because I have trusted my burden to One who is able to bear it.

If I fail to trust Him, I simply pick that burden right back up again, and my actions say I don't believe He has heard me. I then proceed to drag it around behind me, growing more and more weary by the moment. When we refuse to trust, we weigh ourselves down with worry and trying to fix problems ourselves. We don't soar; we sink.

How we need to remember that our God *is* trustworthy. When we lay our burdens at His feet, we can trust that He *is* at work. When we wake up in the morning and give Him our day, we can know that He *will* guide us through each moment—the good and the bad—holding our hands and directing us. Trust is a much more peaceful place to be than fear and doubt.

One of the best ways for me to build a habit of trusting God is to join with other women in prayer and Bible study. When I surround myself with "those who trust in the Lord," my own faith is strengthened. I'm emboldened. May God give us faith today that will "soar high on wings like eagles." May we "run and not grow weary . . . walk and not faint," as together we seek God. May He use this devotional book to deepen our trust in Him.

Father, help us trust You today and find new strength as we remember You are more than able to carry our loads. In Jesus' Name, Amen.

· · · · · · · · · · · · ·

GOING DEEPER
For those days when you have more time to ponder

Read 1 Kings 17:7-16.

What was the burden the widow carried?

When Elijah asked her to bake him a loaf of bread first, how was that a test in trust?

Just as the widow's strength was renewed when she trusted God's prophet, in what areas do you need to let go and trust God today, giving Him your burden?

· · · · · · · · · · · · ·

RESPONDING TO HIS WORD

Day 70

LAVISH LOVE

How great is the love the Father has lavished on us, that we should be called children of God! And that is what we are! —1 John 3:1a

• • • • • • • • • • • • • • • • • •

I love the word *lavish*. "Bestowing profusely . . . produced in abundance . . . marked by profusion or excess," says the Merriam-Webster Dictionary. If something is lavished on you, you are practically buried in it.

My grandmother had a way of lavishing food on me. "Would you like seconds?" she would say, and before I could answer, she was ladling more on my plate again even before I could get the words out, "No, thank you." Oh, wow. This did not help my weight loss plan. However, I see a really fun picture of God, ladling more and more love into my life. "Have some more, Sharon." Oh, what good news that our Father is not stingy with His love! The number of Bible passages that communicate how dearly He loves us are *themselves* lavishly abundant.

Do you feel lavishly loved? Take a moment to sit and meditate on the amazing verse printed above. We who are sinful and weak and fickle have been adopted into God's forever family. Despite our mess-ups, our flaws, our foolishness, even our blatant sins, God has invited us to be a part of the family as His beloved children. He gives to us the full rights:

To enter boldly into His Presence—King of kings—without waiting for permission, because we are His own kids. (See Hebrews 4:16 and Romans 8:15-17.)

To ask Him confidently for all our needs and desires. (See 1 John 5:14.)

To inherit eternal life, entering and living in a place He has prepared for us in His Kingdom. (See John 3:16 and 14:2-3.)

Now, that is lavish, undeserved, ladled-until-it-spills-over-the-plate-onto-the-tablecloth love. No wonder John spoke in exclamation points when he marveled over this truth. May God ladle that love out to you in abundance as you spend time with Him today *lavishly*.

Father God, thank You for Your generous, overwhelming, lavishly ladled-out love for us. What a marvel to be loved by You. We don't deserve it. We can't earn it. We can only sit, open-mouthed, as You continue to love us. We love You, too, Lord. Help us to love You more and more. In Jesus' Name, Amen.

• • • • • • • • • • • • • •

GOING DEEPER
For those days when you have more time to ponder

Read Psalm 136.

Why do you think the psalmist repeated the refrain, "His love endures forever" over and over?

Write that phrase down where you will see it frequently this week. Memorize it. Whisper it as you go about your day. Let it steady and anchor you.

Choose a favorite verse in Psalm 136. Why did that one stand out to you?

• • • • • • • • • • • • • •

RESPONDING TO HIS WORD

Day 71

DO NOT FRET

Be still before the LORD and wait patiently for him; do not fret when men succeed in their ways, when they carry out their wicked schemes. —Psalm 37:7

. . . .

I've been pondering the word *fret*. The Google Dictionary defines fretting as "a state of anxiety or worry." If I'm in an anxious or worried state, then I'm *residing* with worry, right there, all the time. Worried thoughts ping and bounce around in my brain without pause or reprieve. Speaking as an expert from past experience living in this worried state, I particularly love the encouragement this psalm gives those who struggle with fretting:

Do not fret when men . . . carry out their wicked schemes. The teaching is clear: Don't fret. Yep, it sure looks like the bad guys are winning. We see evil parading in mass shootings or another horror story from the sex slave trade. We look at pictures of starving children in refugee camps, suffering because of their own countrymen fighting each other for power. Just watching the news can be terrifying and overwhelming. But guess what? Fretting will not fix it. In fact, evil smiles when we give way to fear. We become secondary victims in our fretful response to evil. Instead, let us, you and me, be adversaries of unrighteousness through prayer, coming before the Lord and battling for what is right and good. We can triumph by our response to evil. This verse tells us how.

Be still before the LORD. Notice that just being still is not enough. No, when we are fretting with our thoughts endlessly churning, stillness is practically impossible. We are instructed to be still *before the LORD.* It is when we consciously come before the Lord Almighty and wait patiently before *Him* in worship and trust that the peace comes. Ponder this powerful quotation from Arthur S. Roche that has helped me remember that worry does no good—and is actually harmful:

"Worry is a thin stream of fear trickling through the mind. If encouraged, it cuts a channel into which all other thoughts are drained."

Wait patiently for Him. To our stillness, we must add patience. We can't simply stop fretting for ten seconds and expect that we'll be all better. No, we're told to wait patiently. This implies that God will answer—but it might not be fast. We can rest in the knowledge that He is good and faithful. We can stay in that waiting and hopeful state until the answers come. And come they will. We know who triumphs in the end.

I wish you, dear one, a fret-free day, today, and times of stillness with the One who holds the universe in His hands.

Father God, forgive me for every wasted, fret-filled minute I have spent. Help me, instead, to fight back through prayer when events and situations are frightening. Help me to be still before You, Mighty God, waiting patiently for You, trusting that You will show me what to pray, what to do, how to respond. Help me to first come to You. In Jesus' Name, Amen.

- - - - - - - - - - - - - - - -

GOING DEEPER
For those days when you have more time to ponder

Read Psalm 37.

The psalmist gives a wealth of wisdom to those who fret when evil seems to be winning. Write out his counsel.

What verse resonates most with you? Write it out.

What current world or personal situation causes you to fret? Write a prayer, right now, right here, asking God to intervene.

RESPONDING TO HIS WORD

Day 72

DON'T JUST LISTEN...DO

Do not merely listen to the word, and so deceive yourselves. Do what it says. —James 1:22

I suffered a vicious neck injury brought on by . . . my own foolishness. Sigh. Chatting on the phone with a friend one day, I decided I should multitask and do some crocheting on my grandson's afghan. So . . . for about half an hour, I held the phone between my good ear and my shoulder and crocheted away, ignoring the increasing discomfort. My body tried hard to tell me that what I was doing to it was not good, but I ignored the pain warnings and continued to chat.

The result: a trip to the ER in the middle of the night. Yikes! Several days and many doses of Advil later, I started to feel better. I guess this older woman can no longer prop a phone between head and ear like she used to. Why, oh why, didn't I listen to those first small signs of discomfort and straighten my neck?

How often, I wonder, do I miss what God is telling me—and how often do I get myself into trouble by not listening? Each of His commands truly is for my good. Ignoring them will, over time, create huge problems. James warns us: Don't just *listen* to the Word of God, actually make wise choices *based* on the Word of God. If we merely nod when we read or hear how God intends us to live, and we continue in disobedience, we are deceiving ourselves.

How much wiser to listen and then change my behavior as soon as I perceive the Holy Spirit's nudge. Poor decisions in my past, when I ignored those warnings, resulted in three important life lessons. Don't allow these thoughts to fill your brain:

Comparison. When I compare myself with others, one of two things result. Either I puff myself up, because I feel "better" in some area, or I wallow in feelings of inadequacy, because someone else is clearly doing it better. Allowing comparison to overtake my thoughts leads to either a prideful attitude or

jealousy, depending on whether I feel superior or inferior. How about I just be me and do the job God has assigned me, without bothering to compare at all? That's a wise choice.

Bitterness. When I have been treated unfairly or unkindly, I need to quickly stop all bitter and resentful thoughts toward the one who has wounded me. Bitterness yields throbbing pains of anger, hurt, resentment, and misery and can grow like cancer. Only when I'm willing to forgive, just like Jesus forgave those who were torturing Him, can God set me free.

Self-pity. This little emotion is deadly. When not immediately cut off, it grows into depression. Dwelling on thoughts about "how hard my life is" and "how terrible it is being me," only yields sadness and increased darkness. Self-pity is the antithesis of thankfulness, and the results of wallowing in self-pity are grim.

Father, thank You for Your Spirit within me, who warns me when my mind strays to places that will hurt me. Help me to listen to Your voice immediately, Lord, and turn from emotions and thoughts that will yield only pain. Forgive me when I fail to listen to Your voice. In Jesus' Name, Amen.

• • • • • • • • • • • • •

GOING DEEPER
For those days when you have more time to ponder

Read Psalm 19.

Psalm 19 describes ways God's Word is a blessing. List them.

Ask yourself, where do I need help in my thought life? Is it comparison, bitterness, self-pity, or another pitfall? What steps can I take to keep my mind focused on what is good?

Find a scripture that will combat those thoughts that threaten to enter your mind and "live there." Write it out, and then pray using that scripture. Ask God to help you refuse thoughts that lead you away from Him.

RESPONDING TO HIS WORD

Day 73

WAGING WAR THROUGH PRAYER

For though we live in the world, we do not wage war as the world does. The weapons we fight with are not the weapons of the world. On the contrary, they have divine power to demolish strongholds. —2 Corinthians 10:3-4

• • • • • • • • • • • • • • • •

I was on a plane returning from a trip to California. After a week-long conference, I was tired. As I sat in the window seat—my favorite—I was hoping my seatmates wouldn't want to chat. I know. Not the most spiritual of attitudes. My heart was not soft toward the one who might sit beside me. I just wanted quiet.

Two college guys joined me, obviously returning from a week of spring break. They were quite involved in their own conversation, so I thankfully opened my book and began to read. After a little while, they stopped talking and started looking at something on a phone that they obviously did *not* want me to see. I started to feel super uncomfortable. I didn't know what they were looking at, but I had a strong sense it wasn't good. And so, I prayed.

You see, as Christians, we don't fight with normal weapons. When we encounter something wrong, we don't have to panic or live with discomfort. We can pray. I turned toward the window, closed my eyes, and began to pray in earnest for the two young men beside me. I asked God to stop them, if I was right in thinking that they were looking at images they shouldn't see. I prayed for their salvation. I asked God to rescue them from darkness and bring them into His great light. All of a sudden, I was energized by God's Spirit and grace alone to wage war for the souls of those two young men. Wow. God seemed to invade my prayers.

When I finished praying, I noticed that the phone was off, and both guys had their eyes closed. Resting. Cool. I opened my book again, and began to read. It was Randy Alcorn's fascinating book on heaven. About an hour later, the guy next to

me woke up and noticed the title of the book. Lo and behold, he started asking me questions about it.

Because of the time spent in prayer, I was ready to talk, my weariness long gone. I was stunned and amazed that God prompted this young man to ask questions about Christ and heaven and life after death. We had an amazing discussion. He told me he wasn't religious, but had been thinking maybe he should look into it. As it turned out, I actually happened to know a senior at his college who runs a Christian forum. He knew about the forum! Said he would check it out. A huge door opened for me to share a bit of the gospel with him. Wow. I am convinced that when we pray . . . God moves. Things happen in the heavenly realms. Oh, if we but had eyes to see the strongholds that are demolished because we asked the God who is *able* to demolish them.

> The one concern of the devil is to keep the saints from prayer. He fears nothing from prayerless studies, prayerless work, prayerless religion. He laughs at our toil, mocks at our wisdom, but trembles when we pray.
> — Samuel Chadwick

Father God, thank You for Your love for those who do not know You. Even now, Lord, I pray for that young man on the plane, that he would know You as Lord and Savior of his life. Use us to wage war against the enemy and his schemes. Use us, through prayer, to demolish strongholds. You are mighty, Father, and You are able to overcome all odds. Thank You for giving us a role, through prayer, to engage the battle as well. In Jesus' Saving Name, Amen.

· · · · · · · · · · · · · · · · · ·

GOING DEEPER
For those days when you have more time to ponder

Read 2 Corinthians 10:1-5 and Ephesians 6:10-20.

What do you learn about the battle from these verses?

Study the references to prayer in both texts. What do you learn about God's power through prayer?

Time to battle: Pray for someone right now who needs to know the saving grace of Christ and who needs to be freed from the enemy's strongholds. May God *move* as you pray, dear one.

. . . .

RESPONDING TO HIS WORD

Day 74

RANDOM THINGS I'M THANKFUL FOR

In the past, he let all nations go their own way. Yet he has not left himself without testimony: He has shown kindness by giving you rain from heaven and crops in their seasons; he provides you with plenty of food and fills your hearts with joy. —Acts 14:16-17

Robert Louis Stevenson wrote a tiny poem in a children's book that I've never forgotten. As a little child, I read: "The world is so full of a number of things, I'm sure we should all be as happy as kings." Now as an adult, I realize a flaw or two in that poem. For starters, I suspect kings are not nearly as happy as we think they ought to be. Always battling that pesky feeling that someone is after their crowns, and then that whole business of running a country probably doesn't very often lend itself to noticing a world "full of a number of things." However, I remember thinking how right Stevenson was. Just look at the world and all that's in it! How much there is to be thankful for—including these weird but happy things that spring to my mind:

My mattress. I was reading a book the other night that described someone sleeping on a hard floor wrapped in a sweater totally insufficient to give warmth. Suddenly, I was grateful for my mattress. Granted, it's nearly ten years old and will eventually need replacing, but it's *not* the floor. It's soft and holds me up, and there are sheets and blankets on top of it. I'm as cozy as can be.

Taking my dog out late at night. I have to admit that when I first received my surprise puppy late one November in *cold* New Hampshire, taking her out and training her was perhaps not a thankful thing, especially since she needed to go out *All. The. Time.* But guess what happens outside at 10:30 pm? The moon and the stars happen. I noticed them again. I'm ashamed to say how long it had been since I'd looked up, up, and up at the vast sky with thousands of tiny lights and the

soft glow of the moon. Wow. Not to mention that I was wrapped in a warm coat—another thing I'm very grateful for in New Hampshire winters. Late night walks with my dog yield views of God's handiwork I would have missed. These days, I often look at the night sky, and it's breathtaking.

The Andy Griffith Show. I know. Weird. The fact is I actually intensely dislike modern television. (Don't get me started . . . this is a thankful devotion.) When Dad Gamble lived with us, he loved television, and we found a common interest in good old Andy. Dad needed eye drops dispensed at 10-minute intervals before bed every night. I used to go in and out, in and out, of his room administering the drops—*before* we discovered Andy Griffith. That show made it easy for me to simply sit on down, crochet a baby blanket, and give Dad a drop every commercial. Hey! I guess I'm thankful for commercials, too. They were natural breaks for Dad's drops. Now, whenever I miss Dad, I find myself watching Andy Griffith and crocheting. It brings back the sweetest memories.

Breathing. Pretty basic, huh? But have you ever heard a loved one struggling to breathe? Heart rending. I'm so very thankful that my body is able to breathe without even thinking about it. I'm grateful for legs and arms that work and hands that grasp and one ear that hears. Yes, I only have one good ear, but I'm thankful that the working ear has more than compensated so I hardly notice a hearing loss.

Leisure. If you're reading this, you have at least some. Leisure, free time, spare time, time off. I realize with great sadness that too many folks on this planet have little or no free time. Every moment is spent seeking or earning food, shelter, water. Life is reduced to survival. What an incredible gift to have leisure time. Time to admire God's beautiful world "so full of a number of things."

I hope God helps you notice the weird and random things that are really great and good gifts from Him. Every bite we take, every sip we drink, every air molecule we breathe . . . is because of our giving and gracious God who has shown kindness by giving rain from heaven and crops in their seasons.

Dear Lord, open our eyes to see Your bounty. You have given abundantly to all of us. The air we breathe, the stars we see, are gifts to every person on earth. And You provide so much more besides. Help us to be a grateful people, noticing Your generosity at every turn. In the Name of Jesus, Greatest of Gifts, Amen.

GOING DEEPER
For those days when you have more time to ponder

Read Acts 14.

What was the context of our theme verses, Acts 14:16-17?

At the end of this chapter, Paul is full of enthusiasm for all God has done through him and Barnabas. List some of the trials Paul went through just in this chapter—and marvel that he still maintains joy and thankfulness.

List some of the "random things" you're thankful for.

. . . .

RESPONDING TO HIS WORD

Day 75

GOD AND AIRPLANES

There is no one like the God of Jeshurun, who rides on the heavens to help you and on the clouds in his majesty. The eternal God is your refuge, and underneath are the everlasting arms. —Deuteronomy 33:26–27a

I was accustomed to traveling by plane. My mother is British, so, as a child, our family often flew to visit my grandparents in England. Later, as an adult, my husband's military assignments took us to Germany and also back to England again. However, once he retired, a significant amount of time passed before we took another trip by plane. Not to mention that in the meantime, terrorists on commercial airlines had brought the World Trade Center towers crashing down. As a result, travel by air was now harder for me to think about.

When I read the verses above from the ancient book of Deuteronomy, I was amazed and encouraged. Who would've thought I'd find an "airplane verse"? But, there it was. These verses are taken from Moses' last words to Israel, blessing them as God's people. What a beautiful passage of Scripture celebrating our mighty God. Let's take a closer look together—and may we be filled with thankfulness:

There is no one like Him. Truly, in all the universe there is no God like our God. He is the one and only God, the maker of heaven and earth. Remembering this is a very good place to begin.

The God of Jeshurun is our God. Jeshurun is "a poetical name for the people of Israel, used in token of affection, meaning, 'the dear, upright people'" (Easton's Bible Dictionary). Because God grafted us in and adopted us as His very own, this phrase refers to us as well. Whether we were born Jewish or not, we can receive this very personally. He is *our* God, and we are dear to Him.

God rides on the clouds. Have you ever gazed from the window seat of a plane, admiring the clouds? Amazing puffs of air and water in the most fantastical arrangements and designs. God rides on those clouds. The next time you marvel at clouds, think about Him riding "in His majesty." King. Fully in charge, fully capable. Take heart from this thought if you are a fearful flyer.

God is the eternal God. The One Moses spoke of is still riding clouds today.

God is our refuge. Do you need a place to hide, a place of safety? Just be where God is. And God is everywhere, including in the sky.

Underneath are the everlasting arms. Consider what is beneath you as you fly. His everlasting arms. God holds you and cradles you wherever you are, His beloved one. You can rest in that.

Whether you are fearful of airplane travel or not, isn't it wonderful to be reminded of our God who is with us *wherever* we go? This little passage of Scripture has enabled me to fly with joy. He is right there with me and underneath are His everlasting arms. Even in the very worst case—an airplane disaster—I would be carried in those arms to life eternal with Him. When we are His, life always has a happy ending.

Heavenly Father, thank You for the safety You provide. You truly are the only refuge, the only safe place in this scary world. Thank You for loving us and providing us with words of great comfort. How thankful we are to be Yours. In Jesus' Name, Amen.

. . . .

GOING DEEPER
For those days when you have more time to ponder

Read Deuteronomy 33.

Choose a favorite verse and write it out.

Write your thoughts to the Lord in response to that verse.

If plane flights are hard for you, copy out Deuteronomy 33:26-27 on an index card to keep with you next time you fly. Or, if you know someone who struggles with plane flights, bless them with this verse, written years before the airplane was even dreamed of and yet bringing comfort and encouragement down through the centuries.

• • • • • • • • • • • • • • • •

RESPONDING TO HIS WORD

Day 76

THREE RESOLUTIONS FOR LIFE

He has shown you, O mortal, what is good. And what does the LORD require of you? To act justly and to love mercy and to walk humbly with your God. —Micah 6:8

. . . .

Sometimes we get more complicated with our resolutions than we need to. This year, consider the advice of Micah, prophet of God, who speaks God's very words to us. For He has shown us what is good and what is required:

To Act Justly.

Help me, Lord, not to play favorites, but to treat difficult folks with the same standard I accord to easy-going individuals.

Show me causes worth supporting in which godly people are working toward justice for those who are oppressed.

Guard my mind when I'm tempted to take shortcuts for my own benefit . . . on taxes or under-tipping or not reporting a mistake made in my favor. Keep me scrupulously fair with others, living above reproach.

Help me to confess when I'm wrong, never letting others take the blame for my actions—even when no one would know. For You, dear Lord, would know.

To Love Mercy.

Help me to show mercy to those who need it most, whether they are easy to love or not.

Remind me, when I drive, to willingly allow other drivers to enter my lane, to be gracious to those who seem to be in a hurry, believing the best of them, to offer my parking space to the one so eager to take it from me.

Remind me of Your mercy to me when I want to hold on to bitterness or unforgiveness.

Give me eyes to see the "why" behind perceived hurts and wounds from another's words.

Show me who needs extra kindness, and give me the grace to pour out love on them.

To Walk Humbly With Your God.

Lord, I want to walk with You, yoked with You, to do the work You've chosen for me. Keep me in step with You.

Show me when my pride and self-centeredness are getting in the way of listening to You and seeking Your wisdom.

Help me to know You more and more, so that I become less and less the center of my own thoughts and actions and You become my focus and my joy.

Remind me, Lord, that I am Yours. My God, who chose me . . . who loves me despite knowing all about me . . . who wants me to be His.

Dear Lord, this year, and every year, help me to act justly and to love mercy and to walk humbly with You. In Jesus' Name, Amen.

. . . .

GOING DEEPER
For those days when you have more time to ponder

Read Micah 6.

This is a sad chapter. God is terribly grieved at the sinful hearts of His people. First, He asks what He has done to deserve such treatment and lists the ways He has been kind to Israel. List those ways here, and then list a few ways He has been kind to you.

Next, God speaks of the worthlessness of an offering when the one bringing it has no heart for God. It's in this context that our verse of the day appears. In what ways do we give only a lip-service sacrifice? What does God require of us?

Lastly, God threatens punishment for His people's disobedience. Today, we don't live as that special nation, but we are grafted together and united by our faith in Christ. God handles our disobedience differently. Read Galatians 6:7. What are some examples of sin that bring their own natural punishment? Read 1 Peter 2:23-25. What is the biggest difference of all because of Christ?

RESPONDING TO HIS WORD

Day 77

FOCAL POINT

Therefore, since we are surrounded by such a great cloud of witnesses, let us throw off everything that hinders and the sin that so easily entangles. And let us run with perseverance the race marked out for us, fixing our eyes on Jesus, the pioneer and perfecter of faith. —Hebrews 12:1–2a

• • • • • • • • • • • • • • • • • •

It often happens during the most innocuous of circumstances. This time, I'm relaxed in my overstuffed chair reading a magazine. The hum begins in my right ear and then increases in fullness and intensity. I know what to do. This isn't my first rodeo. I breathe deeply, slowly. I wait to see if this will be a minor attack or a major Ménière's episode. It's major this time. The pressure builds and flows across my brain. The volume of the hum increases, and then the horizon tilts, the room threatens to spin in ever-tightening, rapid circles, and I feel hot and flushed.

I've already found my focal point. It's a spot on the ceiling to the right of the light. I steel myself to take slow breaths, to remember that this is just an episode. It will pass. I stare at that small spot on the ceiling as if my life depended on it, willing my eyes to focus *Right There*, ignoring the rushing-whirling-tilting thing happening in my inner ear. Ten minutes. Sweating, waiting, breathing, focused on a tiny dot, and the pressure begins to subside, the fullness eases, the hum decreases. I'll be shaky for another half hour or so, but I'm okay. That tiny spot on the ceiling was my key to successfully riding out the attack.

What that little spot on the ceiling was to my physical well-being, the Bible says Jesus is to my spiritual well-being—and yours. *He* is our focal point. We have a calling, and it's to run a particular race that is all ours, staying on the path God has laid out for us. We can be relaxed and at ease on our path when suddenly everything's disrupted, like my Ménière's attack.

What happens when we are blindsided by trouble we didn't expect? Relationships that sour without a warning? What happens when we are tempted to step off our race path and wander toward an enticement that would feed our flesh but ruin our soul? How easy it is to be hindered and entangled. An attack threatens to spin us out of control.

Hebrews tells us to *fix our eyes on Jesus*. Just keep looking at Him no matter what. Don't allow the spinning sensation that everything is falling apart to distract you. Don't give in to panic when life throws you a curve. Steadily, fixedly, unwaveringly, keep your eyes on Jesus, the One and Only, who can and will steady you in uncertain times.

In reality, Jesus is the only point of stillness in a spinning world. He alone does not change. Friends and family can change . . . grow ill . . . die. Homes can be swallowed up by earthquakes and floods. Money saved can be lost. The *only* fixed point is Christ. Shepherd. Light of the World. Savior. Master. Friend. The Way, the Truth, the Life. Living Water. Son of God. God in Flesh. Lover of our Souls. Rescuer. Lord of lords. King of kings.

When we focus on Him . . . the spinning stops.

Dear Lord Jesus, help me to keep my eyes fixed on You in good times and in bad. Oh, how I thank You that You do not change. You are the same yesterday, today, and tomorrow. I choose to look to You for strength and comfort and direction. You are my focal point in a shifting world. I love You, Lord. Amen.

. . . .

GOING DEEPER
For those days when you have more time to ponder

Read Isaiah 9:1-7.

Isaiah was given many glimpses of the Savior, Jesus, Messiah. As you study these verses, write down what you learn about Jesus from them.

Choose your favorite verse from these scriptures, and write it out.

Take time to pray, thanking God for Jesus, your Savior.

- - - - - - - - - - - - - - -

RESPONDING TO HIS WORD

Day 78

WAITING

Now there was a man in Jerusalem called Simeon, who was righteous and devout. He was waiting for the consolation of Israel, and the Holy Spirit was upon him. It had been revealed to him by the Holy Spirit that he would not die before he had seen the Lord's Messiah. —Luke 2:25-26

Do you remember waiting for Christmas? When we were children and had lived five or six whole years, the time from one Christmas to the next represented about a fifth or sixth of our lives. The wait went on forever. Now, of course, a year is a much smaller fraction of my life, so I feel like I barely put the decorations away, and, yikes, it's Christmas again.

Many things in life we await with longing. I longed to be married to Ray Gamble, and then I longed to have children. When I see the suffering and illnesses of dear friends, I particularly long for the day when Jesus will return and wipe away every tear from our eyes.

It's amazing to me how often God's special loved ones are asked to wait. Abraham had to wait over 25 years for the birth of his promised son. The Israelites were in Egypt 400 years before Moses led them to freedom, and even then they wandered in the desert another 40 years. Zechariah and Elizabeth waited a very long time before they gave birth to a son, John the Baptist. God used these times of waiting to prepare and equip His loved ones for the tasks He was preparing for them.

I'm not very good at waiting. I want perfect lives for my loved ones—*now*. Even though I know that struggles have made me stronger, even though I know that it has taken years of life lessons to teach me some important truths, somehow I want it all to happen more easily for those I love. Yet, over and over again,

God calls me to pray—and to wait on Him—as He takes a loved one through another time of testing. And He asks me to trust Him, as He works the situation out for great good.

Simeon, in the verse we read today, *waited all his life* for the Messiah to arrive. God did not disappoint him. Hear Simeon's joy and prayer, as he held Jesus, God Himself distilled into a tiny, human baby, "Sovereign Lord, as you have promised, you may now dismiss your servant in peace. For my eyes have seen your salvation, which you have prepared in the sight of all nations: a light for revelation to the Gentiles, and the glory of your people Israel" (Luke 2:29-32).

Be encouraged as you read these words. God *is* faithful, and He *does* have good plans for those who love Him. He works in hearts and lives—*all* our lives. And, through prayer, He has invited us to be part of the process, helping us and our loved ones become all He has planned. I know that God has allowed the trials we all go through and He can, indeed, bring great good and glory from them.

Keep praying, dear one, wait on the Lord, and encourage those you love to persevere. Take heart and remember that God asks many of His special loved ones to wait on Him. His plans are perfect, and we can trust Him.

Dear Father, thank You for these biblical examples of waiting. I don't always understand the "why" of the wait, but I trust You, Lord. You see the big picture and You know how to grow us in faith and character and perseverance. Help me to remain faithful to pray for faith and character and perseverance in the midst of trials, trusting that You are working even then. In Jesus' Name, Amen.

GOING DEEPER
For those days when you have more time to ponder

Read the story of Simeon in Luke 2:21-35.

Why were Joseph and Mary at the temple? What does that tell you about their obedience to God's commands?

We learn a lot about Simeon in these verses. Write down everything the Bible teaches you about this man's character.

Are you or a loved one in a time of waiting? What are you waiting for? How long have you waited? Ask God to give you Simeon-like faith as you continue to pray and wait.

. . . .

RESPONDING TO HIS WORD

Day 79

ANNA'S HOPE

There was also a prophet, Anna . . . She was very old; she had lived with her husband seven years after her marriage, and then was a widow until she was eighty-four. She never left the temple but worshiped night and day, fasting and praying. Coming up to them . . . she gave thanks to God and spoke about the child to all who were looking forward to the redemption of Jerusalem. —Luke 2:36–38

Anna was a woman who never lost hope. Imagine life as a widow after only seven years of marriage. Hard at any time, but in an era when a woman couldn't just go out and get a job, losing a husband meant poverty and hardship. Only seven years with her husband; only seven years enjoying the status that came with marriage. When Anna was a brand-new bride, I doubt she had any idea she would be a widow for over half a century.

Anna likely had no children. Instead of spending her days with children and grandchildren, she lived in the temple, night and day. Was it hard for her when families arrived to offer sacrifices? Did it hurt to see mothers cradling young babies? How easy it would have been for her to grow bitter and question why others gained what she had lost.

Yet, Anna chose to live her life in praise and in constant contact with the living God. Wow. All her life, she looked forward to the redemption of Jerusalem and never gave up hope. Anna didn't look back on all she did *not* have. She didn't sit in a puddle of self-pity and misery groaning about her lot in life. Instead, she worshiped. She fasted and prayed. She served her living, loving God. And she looked forward to the Redeemer who would come.

At the end of her life, God gave her the incredible, amazing, personal joy of seeing His Son, in the flesh, newly born . . . ready to usher in salvation. How beautiful is that!

On those days when I'm not particularly fond of my circumstances, it helps me to remember Anna. What will I do with my own life disappointments? How will I react when things don't go the way I wish? If I want to please my Heavenly Father and walk in His joy, I will never give up hope. I will *choose* worship, fasting, praying, and giving thanks. May God bless you, dear one, with the *joy* that comes from looking forward with hope to the time when our Savior returns. Just like Anna did.

Heavenly Father, how I would love to meet Anna in Heaven one day. I'd love to hear her story and catch a glimpse of what it was like to hold Your Son, God-made-flesh, in the temple where she had lived for so many years. Thank You, Lord, for the beautiful happy ending You have prepared for me and for all who love You. My hope is safely secured in You. In the Name of Jesus, the Redeemer, Amen.

GOING DEEPER
For the days when you have more time to ponder

Read Romans 5:1-9.

What do you learn from Paul in Romans 5 about a Christian's sure hope?

Does Anna inspire you? In what ways would you desire to be like her?

What gives you *hope* even when life is hard? Is there a scripture verse you cling to when hope is hard to find?

RESPONDING TO HIS WORD

Day 80

ARE YOU LISTENING?

I love the LORD, for he heard my voice; he heard my cry for mercy. —Psalm 116:1

• • • • • • • • • • • • • • •

There were four of us children, and we had lively family dinners to put it mildly. One night, when I was fourteen and my youngest brother was four, our father decided to secretly tape a dinner conversation. He wanted to help us hear how we sounded. All four of us were talkers, and, oh, the noise we made. Our conversations were loud and happy as our excited voices spilled over each other's. I remember it as quite glorious, but perhaps our dad thought differently.

After dinner, Dad revealed the hidden tape recorder and played back our dinner chatter. We were all surprised to hear a tiny four-year-old voice repeatedly asking, "Please pass the salt." No one had paid the remotest attention to that little request. He continued to ask for the salt. (He must have thought dinner needed spicing up.) After several quiet requests, a suddenly very loud and angry four-year-old shouted, *"Please pass the salt!"*

The table grew suddenly silent, and then my poor little brother was berated by all of us for shouting instead of asking quietly and politely. Yikes! Dad was right. We *did* need to hear ourselves at the dinner table. A tiny little boy was vindicated, and we all learned a lesson in the need to *listen* as well as talk.

Have you ever felt like my little brother? Does it seem sometimes that no one at all is listening to you? When we feel that no one hears us, we conclude that no one cares. This isn't always true. We all loved the four-year-old who just wanted the "salt, please," but we didn't show that love by noticing him. It's a good life lesson. One of the most significant ways a person feels valued and loved is when they feel they are being heard.

That's why the verse above struck me so powerfully, "I love the LORD, for he heard my voice; he heard my cry for mercy." God hears us when we cry out to Him.

Every. Single. Time. It's one of the many signs of His great love for us. We never have to feel alone or ignored. Our great God is right there, listening, and loving us. He hears our voices. He hears your voice.

Father, thank You that You care for me, and You hear every cry of my heart. Forgive me when I am too busy talking to listen to You—and to others. Make me sensitive to this, Lord. Teach me to listen. In Jesus' Name, Amen.

GOING DEEPER
For those days when you have more time to ponder

Read Psalm 116.

The psalmist was enduring distress and sorrow. Write out all you learn about his troubles from this psalm.

What is his response to God's rescue?

Which verse in this psalm resonates most with you? Write it out and then respond to God in prayer.

RESPONDING TO HIS WORD

Day 81

INVISIBLE

Whoever oppresses the poor shows contempt for their Maker, but whoever is kind to the needy honors God. —Proverbs 14:31

. . . .

Yes, I know it's pretty ragged. And probably needs to be washed more often than it is, but I'm afraid it will fall apart. The zipper is coming unmoored and needs to be sewn back into place. It's splotchy in spots and decidedly unattractive. But it is warm. Super warm. When you live in New England and you love walking outdoors in below freezing weather, warm trumps attractive. At least that's what I believed one February day when I put this jacket on and headed to my favorite ocean town.

The day started out beautifully. It was a Sweet Selah Day for me: a day set apart for just God and me. I drove to the ocean with a light heart in my warm, weathered jacket. When I arrived, I pulled on a hat that covers my entire head and wraps around my neck. I put on my woolen mittens and headed out for a brisk walk by the ocean. It was about 16 degrees outside, but did that bother me? Not. At. All. My jacket and I were just fine, thank you. I prayed as I walked and even sang out loud because, not surprisingly, no one else was walking the path by the ocean that day. Imagine that!

At the end of the pathway stand gorgeous resort hotels, one after another, all with spectacular views of the crashing waves. I wondered how expensive a room might be for just one night, and if some year my husband and I could sneak away, off-season, and actually stay in one of those ocean-viewing rooms. I decided to hike up to one of the resort offices and ask. Why not?

When I entered the lobby, one person was ahead of me, and I waited my turn. The hotel clerk was attentive and charming to the lady before me. I realized I still had my hat on, so took it off and ran my fingers through my hair. Once that lady was served, the clerk looked at me for about half a second and then turned

away and made a phone call. He did not ever look at me again, or respond when I said a timid, "Excuse me?" It was as if I was not there. I waited a long time and then gave up.

I wandered out, a bit confused, and made my way to a public restroom. And that's when I looked in a mirror and saw myself. Yikes! The jacket was its scruffy self as always, but my hair. Oh dear. The hat had done horrible things to it, and it was standing up in odd peaks all over my head. My face was bright red from the cold and the wind. In short, I looked like a homeless person who had no access to things like mirrors. I began to understand why the man at the hotel had ignored me and not even glanced my way.

Then I became very sad. I was still "me" inside my jacket and messy hair. I was polite and friendly when I spoke to him. In spite of that, because of my appearance, I was a nonentity. Invisible. I might as well not have been there at all.

Lord, I whispered, is this what being homeless and poor feels like? Like you are invisible and just don't count? It was sobering. Convicting. Turning away and acting like someone's not there is usually done in our culture out of fear and ignorance. We don't know this person who doesn't look like us. They might be dangerous. I have been that hotel clerk. Not overtly rude, but absolutely unwilling to engage another human being because of his appearance.

Our God is not like this. Jesus was the poor. He had no place to lay His head most nights and often slept outside. He chose to identify with the ones who are invisible. In our verse above, He declares that honoring Him means being kind to the needy.

Oh, Father, forgive me when I judge by outward appearance alone. Help me to notice and value all human beings, giving special attention, concern, and kindness to the needy. Thank You for that glimpse into what it feels like to be judged based solely on appearance. It wasn't fun. Show me, Lord, how to give—not just money—but my time and my attention to those in need. Overcome my fears. In Jesus' Name, Amen.

GOING DEEPER

For those days when you have more time to ponder

Read Isaiah 61.

This glorious proclamation is all about Jesus. (See also Luke 4:18-21.) What do you learn about Jesus from Isaiah 61, who He is and why He came?

How does God feel about the disenfranchised . . . the invisible?

In what ways are you serving the poor? Are any areas of involvement tugging at you as you ponder? Seek God about it. Is there more He would have you do?

• • • • • • • • • • • • • • • •

RESPONDING TO HIS WORD

Day 82

LOVE YOUR ENEMIES

"You have heard it was said, 'Love your neighbor and hate your enemy.' But I tell you, love your enemies and pray for those who persecute you, that you may be children of your Father in heaven. He causes his sun to rise on the evil and the good, and sends rain on the righteous and the unrighteous." —Matthew 5:43-45

Shortly after we moved to New Hampshire, I innocently took my dog on a walk around our new neighborhood. As always, I carried with me two plastic bags to take care of any doggie business that might happen along the way. As I passed a house around the corner and up the hill from mine, I was suddenly accosted by two Very Angry Persons. They came racing out of their house, stood near me on the sidewalk, and berated me for letting my dog mess on their lawn. It was a verbal assault the likes of which I had never experienced before, complete with angry gestures and words one should not use. Yikes.

The truth was, I hadn't done this terrible thing. In fact, my blameless dog and I had just started our walk and nothing of that nature had occurred. I held out my little bags and tried to explain, but the angry words just kept on rolling. At the end of this barrage, the homeowner shouted, *"Go! Just Go!"* I went. I was shaking like a leaf. I don't do well with confrontations, and this was a doozy. Hoo boy.

Perhaps not surprisingly, God had recently been teaching me, in another context, the lesson about loving my enemies and praying for those who persecute me. Evidently, He decided I needed more practice. So, as I shakily walked toward home, I began praying for this irate couple and asking God to bless them.

As I finished my walk, I heard God's whisper prompting me to bake cookies for them. Really, Lord? Oh, dear me. Bake cookies and knock on their actual door? After they yelled at me and swore at me? "Yes."

Well, God's command seemed very clear, so I baked those cookies and prayed with my family. Making sure I had my phone with me in case they hurt me when I knocked on their door, in fear and trembling, back to their house I went—without the dog.

When I knocked, the lady of the house immediately opened it. She was weeping. I had imagined quite a few possible scenarios in my mind, but never that she would be crying. She was so glad I had come. She was? I was flummoxed. It seems the real culprit was another woman with a similar black dog who passed by them a second time after I had left them in bewilderment. She said it wasn't like her to act the way she had toward me, and she was so embarrassed. Could I forgive her and . . . cookies? Thank you. More tears. I even got a hug. Go figure. What a happy ending—and most unexpected.

Oh, the sweetness and wisdom of the Lord to give us this good word about how to deal with enemies. How foolish it is to allow bitterness to eat us up inside when someone is unkind to us. Usually, unkind people are very unhappy people—and need our prayers far more than they need our defensive and angry responses. As I ponder who my "enemies" are, I realize that often they are people who are hurting. God's good command to love them and pray for them helps heal both of us.

Here's a way we can pray for an enemy. Perhaps you are thinking of someone right now. Put their name into this prayer as we pray together.

Father, reveal Your great love to [name of person]. Whatever wounds he/she carries, please heal them. Show [name of person] that he/she is never too far from You; he/she can always turn back to You. Remind him/her that You look for lost sheep. You run toward the prodigal. You delight to give mercy to all who need it. Help me to show Your love even to my enemies so that my enemy can become my brother or sister in Christ and one day stand before Your throne with me lifting his/her hands high in praise to You, the King. In Jesus' Name, Amen.

GOING DEEPER

For those days when you have more time to ponder

Read Matthew 5.

In verses 1-16, study the Beatitudes and the challenge to be light. What do you learn about the kind of persons Jesus wants us to be? List some of the qualities found in these verses that make us shine for Him.

Now study verses 38-48. Jesus is full of practical teaching on ways to love our enemies and why we are to love them. Summarize His words.

Write a prayer, asking the Lord to help you love and pray for the difficult people ("enemies") in your life.

. . . .

RESPONDING TO HIS WORD

Day 83

TINY FIGHTER

When you go to war against your enemies and see horses and chariots and an army greater than yours, do not be afraid of them, because the LORD your God, who brought you up out of Egypt, will be with you. —Deuteronomy 20:1

. . . .

I was sitting in one of my favorite places. As we did each summer, we were visiting dear friends who happen to have a screened deck that brushes up against beautiful woods. I had tiptoed out there in the early morning stillness for my time with the Lord. Initially, I just basked in the morning sunshine and birdsong. It had been a busy year. The quiet, mixed with forest noises, soothed and comforted. I leaned my head back and thanked God for this little place of respite.

All of a sudden, that peace was interrupted. I sat back up with a start. What was that noise? I heard the ugliest, angriest, little huff. I mean, whatever woodland creature was making this noise was seriously perturbed. Not only jarring, it was a bit disconcerting. And it would *not stop*.

I tried to focus on prayer and Bible reading, but the angry little bluster continued. Finally, I stood up and started looking for the culprit. What a surprise to discover it was just a little sparrow. It had something in its mouth, and it was furious with me. It flew at the screen and huffed and grumbled and puffed out its little chest. Eventually . . . even though I was many times its size and in my favorite spot on the deck . . . I moved. Into the house I went to finish my quiet time in, well, *quiet!*

Later in the day, my friend told me that the sparrow had found a small hole in their screen. This resourceful mama bird had entered the deck and built a nest in a plant pot—that had been hanging directly over my head. Poor little mother bird. She didn't dare come in onto the deck, but, oh, she made it abundantly clear

she wanted me *out*. I was quite impressed with her boldness and her refusal to quit making that awful noise. She loved her babies and had probably just flown out for a quick snack.

You know, sometimes I feel as tiny as that sparrow, fighting against a culture and the enemies of God who are strong and big and entrenched. It can seem as hopeless as it must have seemed to that mama bird watching me sit directly beneath her nest. Right under her babies, maybe still in their eggs needing her warm and protecting body over them. Perhaps, like in the verse above, God fought for her when He moved me back into the house. He notices when sparrows fall to the ground, after all. Right?

The key to winning any battle is remembering *who* is with us, isn't it? We might be tiny fighters trying to speak truth in love to a culture that doesn't like what we are saying, but we don't fight alone. God is able to change circumstances as we pray and ask Him. God is able to change the hearts of the enemies, showing them His love and His truth. God is able to keep us in the battle, not growing weary of the praying and the loving and the standing fast. We don't fight alone, tiny fighter. The God of the Universe goes with us if we belong to Him. Do not be afraid. He can move an enemy as huge as I must have appeared to that sparrow.

Father, give me the tenacity and fervor of that little mama bird, as I fight through prayer and loving words for Your truths in this culture. Remind me of Your Presence. Help me to see the urgency of the need. Help me to be persistent in prayer and service. Help me to enter the battles of Your choosing without fear, knowing that You are with me . . . and the enemy is the tiny one. In Jesus' Name, Amen.

· · · · · · · · · · · · ·

GOING DEEPER
For those days when you have more time to ponder

Read 2 Thessalonians 3.

Paul was writing to people who also lived in an ungodly culture and who also needed to fight forces much larger than they. Find every verse in this chapter that encourages perseverance in the fight.

What challenges you most in this chapter?

What is your biggest fight at the moment? Are you laboring in prayer for one who has drifted? Are you engaged in fighting poverty, or slave trafficking, or some other injustice as an ambassador for Christ? Take a moment now and battle through prayer for whatever fight is on your heart today.

· · · · · · · · · · · · · · · ·

RESPONDING TO HIS WORD

Day 84

PRACTICING TRUST

"Do not let your hearts be troubled. Trust in God; trust also in me." —John 14:1

. . . .

Jesus tells us we are not to let our hearts be troubled, but to trust God instead. How very difficult is that? And yet, it does seem to be a command, not a suggestion. Do *not* let your hearts be troubled. Whoa. How does one go about keeping difficult commands like that?

I propose that, like any other life skill, we must practice. As I pondered this, God reminded me of the way I taught our young daughters to obey a difficult command. When I said, "Come here now," I insisted that they obey. I tried not to give this command unless absolutely needed. Who wants to be interrupted in the middle of a pretend tea party with stuffed animals? Whenever possible, I gave them a warning. However, at times, I needed them to obey and come to me—*now*! They might have wandered too close to a road or too far away in a busy store. I came up with a way to teach them: we *practiced*.

We would gather into a huddle in the kitchen where I shared "The Plan." They would "pretend to play" but secretly wait for my "come here now!" command. When they heard it, they were to race to me, and, if they could do it three times in a row, with playing in between, we would celebrate with an adventure at the park. They loved this practicing game. They would play with one ear ready, and, at the instant they heard my voice, they would come racing into the kitchen. It was especially wonderful to me that this "practice" meant when I called them to come close during times of real danger . . . they obeyed.

It occurs to me that we could practice obedience to this Scriptural command in little ways as well. Then, when a big test comes and trouble surrounds us, we are used to stopping our hearts from worry. We are used to turning to God in trust and prayer.

Let's make a point to ask God, "Remind me to run to You when I'm troubled." Perhaps if we start with our little struggles, like being late for an appointment or not being able to find a certain shirt, we'll train ourselves to immediately trust God. We'll be ready when those times of great distress come into our lives. Perhaps, with practice, going to Him at the beginning of a problem will become an automatic response.

My daughters didn't instantly come to me the first time I called. Or the second time for that matter. I had to teach and train them to come when I called. It took time and practice, but was so worth it knowing my little ones trusted me enough to obey and come *now* for their own safety. Let's not grow discouraged about our troubled hearts. Let's acknowledge the command, *do not let* your heart be troubled, and then practice. Like my girls, it will be easier over time.

Dear Father, help me come to You directly when trouble arises. I need Your help to keep my heart untroubled and trusting. Remind me, Lord, when the first hint of trouble appears, to practice bringing it to You. Oh, how I long for the day when trust is my automatic, grateful response. Thank You for being loving, patient, and merciful with me. In Jesus' Name, Amen.

· · · · · · · · · · · · · ·

GOING DEEPER
For those days when you have more time to ponder

Read John 13:21–14:13.

Why were the disciples troubled? Was this a little trouble or a big one?

What reasons does Jesus give for not letting hearts go to that troubled place?

What is troubling your heart today? Or what is a common worry that stirs you up? Write it down and then write a prayer asking God to help you trust instead.

RESPONDING TO HIS WORD

Day 85

SINGLE-MINDED

I will give them singleness of heart and action, so that they will always fear me for their own good and the good of their children after them. —Jeremiah 32:39

• • • • • • • • • • • • • • • • • • • •

On Columbus Day Monday in 1974, my life changed dramatically. I went roller-skating with a friend of mine, Ray Gamble. He drove me home, and, then, before I opened the car door, he unexpectedly kissed me. I got out of the car and walked right into a bush in my front yard! He had my heart from that day forward. More than forty years later, I still love the guy who kissed me back when I was sweet 16. How blessed I am that my high school sweetheart is my dear husband.

On April 22, 1962, my life changed eternally. As a four-year-old, I knelt at the side of my mother's bed and prayed asking Jesus into my life. I still remember the *joy* of that moment. I gave my heart to God that day with a love even more profound than the love I have for my husband. God reigns first in my life—my love for Ray is a gift from His hand.

Although Ray and I both have a deep love for God, "singleness of heart and action" for God can be hard at times. We are often more focused on ourselves. We need scriptures like the verse above from Jeremiah to remind us that we can *ask* God to give us single-minded focus. And Jeremiah encourages us that when we stand resolute and steadfast, good will come to us—and good will come to our children.

For their own good. First of all, when God gives us singleness of heart and action, it's for our own good. When we fear Him, bowing in reverence to His Gloriousness and Holiness, we are in the right place. Life is good when we remember who we are and whose we are.

For the good of their children. I find it very interesting and a total God-thing that, in addition to our own good, good will also come to our children. Wow. Talk about a long-term effect from hearts set on God! We want our daughters, sons-in-law, and grandchildren to love the eternal God. When we walk in devotion to the Lord, God tells us in this verse, that our resolute faith works for the good of our children after us. Now that's powerful motivation.

Heavenly Father, please give us "singleness of heart and action," so that we will always fear You. Thank You that You give this not only for our good, but also for the good of our children. Lord, over and over, we see that Your commands are given out of Your great love. We surrender to You our wayward hearts again and again, dear Lord. Mold us for Your glory. In Jesus' Mighty Name, Amen.

. . . .

GOING DEEPER
For those days when you have more time to ponder

Read Jeremiah 32.

What calamity is happening to Israel and why is God allowing it?

In the midst of tragedy, God promises a bright future. List some of the gracious mercies He will give to His people in the future.

Notice Jeremiah's prayer in verses 16-25. What do you learn about prayer in the midst of trial?

. . . .

RESPONDING TO HIS WORD

Day 86

LIKE A CHILD

"Truly I tell you, anyone who will not receive the kingdom of God like a little child will never enter it." And he took the children in his arms, placed his hands on them and blessed them. —Mark 10:15-16

• • • • • • • • • • • • • •

One of my grandsons called me when he was six. First, he asked to talk to the dog, but then had a nice chat with his Nina (me). He invited himself to our house for the summer, assuring me he'd leave when school started. My daughter was hyperventilating in the background and vetoed that idea. She'd like him around for at least most of the summer.

I love it when my grandsons call. When they were little, their conversations were a little harder to decipher. They mangled words in adorable fashion. A sandwich was a *sammich*, a bicycle was a *bikeasaur*, and when they wanted to be picked up, they'd ask, "Hold you?" When my oldest grandson was tiny, he would phone and say, "Nina—song?" That was my cue to sing—and I did with joy. Then he'd say, "More?" And I'd sing another one. This continued indefinitely until his mom finally wanted the phone back. A smile is spreading across my face as I write remembering little boy sweetness.

God tells us to come to Him as little children. Like my grandsons, it's okay if we don't pronounce all the words right. We don't have to be polished and smooth and perfect to gain entrance to His Presence. In fact, we need to shed any pretenses and all pride when we meet with Him. He is our Abba—the Father God who actually wants an intimate relationship with us. It's okay to come to Him like a child. He insists on it. He delights in you even more than a grandparent delights in precious grandchildren.

The prophet Zephaniah celebrates the deep love God has for us with these tender words:

> "The LORD your God is with you,
> the Mighty Warrior who saves.
> He will take great delight in you;
> in his love he will no longer rebuke you,
> but will rejoice over you with singing."
> —Zephaniah 3:17

I have been a Christian many years now, and I can testify that even at the tender age of four, my God was with me. He delighted in little me. And He still does.

Abba Father, help us to remember that You call us Your children. For those of us who have placed our lives in Your hands, that is exactly who we are. Thank You for Your tender care over each one of us. Help us to always run to You and not away from You. Thank You for being the perfect parent to us, Your children. In Jesus' Name, Amen.

. . . .

GOING DEEPER
For those days when you have more time to ponder

Read Mark 10.

Notice in this chapter how dearly Jesus values children—and those who were often neglected in the culture of His day. List examples of those Jesus reached out to that others considered unworthy.

Can you name individuals in your life who are neglected and overlooked?

Pray for them and ask God for His guidance in serving them.

RESPONDING TO HIS WORD

Day 87

WALK THIS WAY

Whether you turn to the right or to the left, your ears will hear a voice behind you, saying, "This is the way; walk in it." —Isaiah 30:21

. . . .

It was the middle of a snowy New England winter. I was driving my parents to Logan airport where they would fly south to visit my brother and his family in Florida. They had long anticipated this trip, and their flight the night before had been canceled due to this snowstorm. We were determined to catch the rescheduled flight.

Unfortunately, the roads were still slushy and gritty from the sanding and plowing the day before, and that slushy grit hit the car's side windows making visibility extremely limited. I'd never seen windows so completely smeared before. I had a very hard time seeing to my right or to my left. This was not a fun drive, especially since most of the way we were on the highway.

About halfway to the airport, an incident occurred that very nearly cost us our lives. The bed of the large truck ahead of us was loaded with tree branches. With no warning, a huge tree limb dropped off the back of the truck right into our lane. I had very little time to make a decision, but that limb didn't seem like anything one would ever choose to drive over!

I looked to my left, and there was a car next to me . . . I could not swerve left. With all that grit plastered on my windows, I couldn't tell what was behind me or to my right . . . so no braking or swerving to the right. Cringing, I steered straight ahead and over the limb we went. The car jolted but stayed in its lane.

In the next instant, an eighteen-wheeler sped by us on the right. Oh. My. Had I swerved to the right, I don't think I would be typing this. My precious mother in the passenger seat would surely have been killed. How thankful I am that we stayed the course, even though it took us over that awful tree limb.

Scary as that was, it was the right thing to do. I'm forever grateful I didn't swerve to avoid that branch.

Oftentimes, staying on the right path out of obedience to the Lord can seem just as scary as that branch appeared to us. He asks us to forgive or to confront someone in sin or to tell the truth when it hurts, and we look wildly about to see if we can swerve and avoid obedience. Yet, the safest way, no matter how hard it looks, is always to stay on His path.

May God bless you today with a hearing heart so that you follow Him even when it's scary. Going off that path? Oh, that's far, far worse. May we gladly follow the good Shepherd who says, "This is the way; walk in it."

Dear Lord, help me to hear Your voice and gladly obey. Keep me always on the right road. In Jesus' Name, Amen.

. . . .

GOING DEEPER
For those days when you have more time to ponder

Read Isaiah 30:9-26.

What did God's children do that demonstrated their rebellion against Him?

What should they have done?

Is it hard for you to stay on God's path? How can you better position yourself to hear His voice saying, "This is the way; walk in it"?

. . . .

RESPONDING TO HIS WORD

Day 88

GOD, GIVER OF SWORDS AND OTHER UNEXPECTED THINGS

"Which of you, if your son asks for bread, will give him a stone? . . . How much more will your Father in heaven give good gifts to those who ask him!" —Matthew 7:9, 11b

One of my favorite duties as "Nina" is to pray for my grandchildren. Over the years, I've witnessed countless sweet answers to prayer for those little ones I love so dearly. I often pray that each one will develop a deep relationship with God.

One of my favorite answers to that ongoing prayer came about when our oldest grandson was two and a half. At that age, he loved to be the one praying before a meal and usually his prayers were pretty much to the point. "Thank You for the food, Amen." But this time, he got down to business about something he really wanted. "Dear God, thank You for our dinner and please help us get some swords."

Ha! Well, why not ask, right? Evidently a sword or two would rock his world. The really sweet thing is this . . . his mother shared his prayer on Facebook, and, quite unexpectedly, a friend wrote back that she had some foam toy swords . . . and was going to bring them over for him. My grandson had asked for a crazy thing—and he got it. Isn't that just so kind of our God?

Throughout the years, I, too, have asked God for some crazy things. Back when our girls were small—and our budget was also small—I prayed for a free piano. I thought perhaps, if I had one, I could teach piano to supplement our income. Within two weeks, right in our church bulletin was an advertisement for a free piano. God said yes to my request, and I happily taught piano lessons for many years.

God also has provided at various times a piano bench, a freezer, funds in just the right amount to pay a bill, free vacations on Cape Cod when a family vacation was totally out of our reach. Oh, the stories I could tell!

Here's the deal. *Ask.* We are God's children. He is a Father who gives good gifts. It's okay to simply ask. Just like any good parent—and God is the very best of parents—if your request isn't right for you, He can close the door. But why not ask Him? You might just get that sword you always wanted.

Father, forgive me when I forget Your goodness as a parent. I know You don't always answer my requests with a yes. Still, You don't mind my asking, and I can trust that You give good gifts. If I ask for bread, You will not give me a stone. Teach me to come to You as a child, asking in trust that You will do what is best. Please, Lord, say no to those requests that will not bring You honor and glory and fulfill Your purposes for my life. Thank You that you allow me to ask. I love You, Abba Father. In Jesus' Name, Amen.

. . . .

GOING DEEPER
For those days when you have more time to ponder

Read Matthew 7.

Describe what Jesus teaches us in this chapter about God's perspective when we ask Him for our needs and wants.

What hinders us from bringing our requests to God for things big and small?

Write a prayer, asking God for one of your heart's desires. Acknowledge His right as Father to answer as He sees best, but go ahead and ask Him and trust His reply.

. . . .

RESPONDING TO HIS WORD

Day 89

THE NECESSITY OF HARDSHIPS

[They were] strengthening the disciples and encouraging them to remain true to the faith. "We must go through many hardships to enter the kingdom of God," they said. —Acts 14:22

. . . .

It was a challenging time in our family. My son-in-law was training for deployment to Afghanistan, and my daughter, his wife, was having a dreadful time trying to figure out childcare. She was about to become a single parent to their two-year-old son, while working full time in Germany. She wondered if I would fly over to Germany and help out. Meanwhile, my dear 90-year-old father-in-law had developed major health issues that required much of my time and care, and I was juggling a job of my own. I felt torn, wanting to "be there" for everyone.

God spoke to me so wonderfully through Luke's words in the verse above, and I had to smile. Paul and Barnabas strengthened and encouraged the flock to stay true to the faith. How? By sharing with them that we must go through many hardships to enter the kingdom of God. At first glance, this hardly seems reassuring. Yet, even in this hard statement, God's Word strengthened and encouraged me that day.

Hardships should not come as a shock. They are normal and enter our lives at random intervals. In fact, according to Paul and Barnabas, adversity is evidently required for our growth and our entrance into God's kingdom. Somehow knowing that God had allowed my particular difficulty at that time, and that furthermore we all must go through trying times to enter His kingdom (which I surely want to do) . . . helped me stay the course.

Satan would love to see us quit when rocky times hit. He would love to see us stop serving, stop reading the Word, stop doing what God has called us to do. I felt a tug toward self-pity and isolation during that time. But think about it.

If hardships are to be a natural part of living, then, of course, we go on living and doing for God's kingdom right in the middle of it all. We still serve. We still gather with believers. We still spend time in God's Word, seeking His direction, asking Him what to stop and what to continue. I grew through that hard time. My need for God's direction pulled me closer to Him, and I learned a bit more in the process. How grateful I am that I didn't quit when the going got rough.

Dear weary one, what hardships are you experiencing? Be strengthened and encouraged. God has a purpose in every single one. Remain true to the faith, and serve Him right in the midst of it all. I suspect that there . . . in the eye of the storm . . . is where we find *joy*, as we trust Him to give us strength for each new day.

Heavenly Father, thank You for the reminder that hardships are allowed by You. In fact, they must happen. Help me to receive what You allow. Show me how to cope, and how to serve You in the midst of trouble. I lean on You. In Jesus' Name, Amen.

. . . .

GOING DEEPER
For those days when you have more time to ponder

Read Hebrews 11.

List those mentioned in this chapter who suffered hardships.

Why do you think God, through Paul and Barnabas, encouraged believers by telling them hardships are a "must"?

Write a prayer, listing your current hardships and asking for strength and encouragement as you walk with God through them.

RESPONDING TO HIS WORD

Day 90

OUR GOD IS HUGE!

*Now I saw heaven opened, and behold, a white horse.
And He who sat on him was called Faithful and True, and
in righteousness He judges and makes war. . . . And He
has on His robe and on His thigh a name written:
KING OF KINGS AND LORD OF LORDS. —Revelation 19:11, 16 NKJV*

I had the privilege of hearing my just-turned-three grandson explain Jesus to me. It was quite the experience. His eyes grew really big as he declared, "Jesus is HUGE! He is very strong, and He is very brave. He carries a sword (said with wide-eyed emphasis!), and He is the very best hero of all."

Gotta love it! This little guy has a sense of awe when he thinks of the Lord Jesus that is altogether fitting and true. Our Savior Jesus is absolutely tender and patient and caring. He loves little children. He even extends to us an amazing privilege—calling us His friends. Yet, He is also HUGE. When He comes on that white horse one day, I suspect there will be a lot of trembling going on, and everyone will bow before the King. My grandson helped me see Jesus in that light—and I'm grateful.

Sometimes I'm guilty of focusing on the "nice and safe" passages about Jesus. I love the way He touched the leper. The way He gathered little children in His arms makes me smile. His tender, kind friendliness to Zacchaeus, the tax collector. These passages of my Savior, my Shepherd, feel safe.

However, this same Jesus is also the Lion of Judah. When He rides that white horse into battle in righteousness and once and for all declares Himself as King of kings and Lord of lords, His wrath and holiness will be on full display. He is so patient with us, not willing that any should perish according to 2 Peter 3:9.

Yet the day will come when He becomes the just Judge of the world. That's HUGE, in my grandson's words. No one will stand against Him on that great and terrible day.

Those of us who know Him will be more than okay. Not because we deserve to be okay. We will be saved because of His blood, poured out on our behalf, and because of His grace, and because we received it. I am beyond thankful. You know what? Even though I favor the passages about Him being my good Shepherd and all . . . part of me is very awfully glad Jesus is HUGE. I do feel safe knowing that.

Heavenly Father, I worship You. You are Holy, Holy, Holy. You are righteous, and Your Son is Faithful and True. Thank You for the promise of justice coming. Thank You that evil will lose. I praise You that You are the Victor. King of kings. Lord of lords. Jesus, Your Name is Mighty. Amen.

GOING DEEPER
For those days when you have more time to ponder

Read Revelation 19.

Describe Jesus as He appears in this chapter.

Reread the section about the bride of Christ and the wedding supper. How does this imagery show you the longing God has for His church?

Write out a prayer, responding to this chapter. Tell Jesus what you don't understand or share with Him your eagerness to be with Him. Be honest and talk to Him about what you read in Revelation 19.

RESPONDING TO HIS WORD

Day 91

TEACH ME

Instruct the wise and they will be wiser still;
teach the righteous and they will add to their learning.
The fear of the LORD is the beginning of wisdom,
and knowledge of the Holy One is understanding. —Proverbs 9:9-10

Ray and I had a hard time communicating when we were first married. We thought so differently. As an example, Ray's idea of a great birthday was to take me shopping and let me choose my own present. That way he was sure I would receive a gift I liked. It was a sensible approach, and he was totally unprepared for my vehement dislike of it. Poor guy.

My idea of a great birthday was way more complex and involved cake and candles, sentimental cards, and surprises wrapped in adorable paper with ribbons and bows. Needless to say, we had some adjusting to do. After a disaster or two in the birthday department, I realized that I needed to *teach* Ray how to give me a happy birthday. And . . . I needed to stop giving Ray surprise presents he didn't want and let him teach me what would actually make him happy on his birthday. We "added to our learning" about each other as we finally became teachable. Birthdays are much nicer nowadays.

A large card sits beside me on my desk that simply reads in big letters: TEACH ME. Its purpose is to remind me that I am to be a lifelong learner. And this doesn't just apply to marriage, although I always have more to learn in that department, for sure. In every relationship I need to be willing to "learn" the other person. How are they wired? What makes them happy? Where are they sensitive? As I learn about the people I know, I'm able to serve them and communicate with them in a better, more meaningful way. When someone is angry or even curt with me, I try to have a "teach me heart" and discover what caused

feelings to be injured. I can tell you, that is much more useful than harboring resentment or bitterness.

As important as it is to learn about others, it's most important that we learn about God. In fact, Proverbs 9 tells us that "the fear of the LORD is the beginning of wisdom, and knowledge of the Holy One is understanding" (v. 10). Our starting point for understanding life is God. Pure and simple. Talk about a lifelong assignment!

Do I read Scripture with the desire to know and understand my Creator better? Do I bring Him my troubles and worries and ask for *His* understanding to guide mine? Am I teachable when it comes to knowing God? For this is the path to wisdom. And this is where to start.

Dear Father, please help me to develop a "teach me heart." Give me a learner's attitude as I approach people and love them. Most of all, dear Lord, help me to know You and love You more and more. In Jesus' Name, Amen.

· · · · · · · · · · · · · · · · · · · ·

GOING DEEPER
For those days when you have more time to ponder

Read Proverbs 9.

List the characteristics of the "simple" ones who are full of folly.

List the reasons wisdom is best.

Choose a favorite verse in Proverbs 9. Write it out and then write a prayer, talking to the Lord about this verse.

· · · · · · · · · · · · · · · · · · · ·

RESPONDING TO HIS WORD

Day 92

MAKING THE MOST OF EVERY OPPORTUNITY

And pray for us, too, that God may open a door for our message, so that we may proclaim the mystery of Christ, for which I am in chains. Pray that I may proclaim it clearly, as I should. Be wise in the way you act toward outsiders; make the most of every opportunity. —Colossians 4:3-5

· · · · · · · · · · · · · · · · ·

It was the summer of 1972, and my family was spending a week in a little cabin by a lake in northern New Hampshire. I was fourteen years old and my sister Bethany was twelve. We had been coming to this particular spot for several years, and Bethany was a fast friend with the owner's daughter (I'll call her Belinda). Shortly after our arrival, Bethany felt convicted that this was the summer Belinda must ask Jesus into her heart.

Bethany was passionate about it . . . but she wanted me to do the talking! She had a sense that I was the one to share. I had no idea how to start a conversation with Belinda, especially since she was really my sister's friend. So, Bethany and I prayed together and asked God to give me an opportunity to talk with Belinda about Christ.

One morning, halfway through our week, I got up early and sat on the dock with my Bible. Belinda saw me there, joined me, and asked what I was doing. I shared with her my love for Jesus, and she accepted Him as her Lord and Savior. Right there on that dock! Quietly and simply, Belinda became a child of God. He had prepared my heart to speak His truth and Belinda's heart to receive it—and my sister's heart to pray. Bethany was ecstatic. We all were! After we returned home Bethany and Belinda stayed in touch all year writing letters.

Summer of 1973 arrived, and, before we were to return to our little cabin, a phone call came from Belinda's parents. Our friend had dived into the ice-cold lake on a very hot day. And died. Evidently, she had a weak heart that no one knew about and the shock was too much. Oh, how we grieved! And . . . oh, how we marveled!

God loved Belinda so much that He gave Bethany a burning passion to tell her about salvation in Jesus Christ. He allowed me to be the vehicle to tell her of His love. Through His prompting, He made sure Belinda would be with Him forever. My sister and I have never forgotten Belinda or the awe we felt as we realized the way God had used us to ensure this child of twelve would spend eternity with Him. That's how much He loves His children.

I believe that God used prayer as the key to open the door of opportunity. He burdened Bethany to pray, and He prepared Belinda to receive eternal life. Paul speaks of this truth in our verse for today, "And *pray* for us, too, that God may open a door for our message, so that we may proclaim the mystery of Christ, for which I am in chains. *Pray* that I may proclaim it clearly, as I should. Be wise in the way you act toward outsiders; make the most of every opportunity" (Colossians 4:3-5, emphasis mine).

Father, thank You for Your deep love for those who do not know You. Help me to make the most of every opportunity You give me, clearly proclaiming the gospel. Use me, Lord, to bring others to You. In Jesus' Name, Amen.

GOING DEEPER
For those days when you have more time to ponder

Read Colossians 4.

What do you learn from this chapter about sharing Christ with others?

Paul lists names of people he loves. Which person intrigues you most and why? What does this listing of names tell you about Paul?

List the people in your life you most want to see come to know Christ. Pray for them now, asking for opportunities and open doors to share.

RESPONDING TO HIS WORD

Day 93

LORD, THIS IS TOO BIG FOR ME

Rescue me from the mire, do not let me sink; deliver me from those who hate me, from the deep waters. —Psalm 69:14

• • • • • • • • • • • • • • • •

I was helping out in the prayer room at a major conference. Women were lined up outside our door just waiting for a turn to sit and pray. Story after story of tragedy and heartache poured out. I could barely grasp the pain many of them were carrying. Some had endured unthinkable suffering. Just hearing their stories . . . I hurt. I remember holding countless hands as I began my prayers over and over again, "Lord, this is too big for me."

Not long afterwards, numerous individuals dear to me were in a similar spot, going through hard times. They were sinking in deep waters, trapped in the mire. My heart would ache and break as I listened to each story. I felt helpless. I can't fix this. I can't make things better. And so, once again, I began my prayers with an acknowledgment of my helplessness, "Lord, this is too big for me."

I find it helpful to remind myself that you and I are not called to solve the problems of the world. Our job is to come *alongside* hurting people, listen to them, love them, and then point them to the only One who has the answers. I suspect that you, too, are often confronted with problems too terrible to bear. Whenever you walk through a trial like that yourself, whenever you walk through it with another, whatever the issue . . . *it is not too big for God.*

Hear His words of reassurance today from the same psalm, "The Lord hears the needy and does not despise his captive people" (v. 33). Whether we are crying out for a wayward child or a spouse or praying with a friend in deep distress or simply grieving at all the evil in this world, it helps to remember that God is able to handle any situation. All we are called to do is simply entrust it to His care. He hears the needy. He does not despise the captive. He rescues.

May God reach down and pull you or your loved ones out of the mire, no matter what you are walking through, dear one. May you be a blessing to others as you bring big troubles to a Bigger God.

Oh, Father, this world is a hard place at times. We are small and unable to fix the messes. How I thank You that You are more than able to help us in times of trouble. How I thank You for Your words, "Fear not, for I am with you" (Isaiah 41:10). Lord, if You are with me, I can cope. Thank You for Your Presence and Your help. In Jesus' Name, Amen.

GOING DEEPER
For those days when you have more time to ponder

Read Psalm 69.

List some of David's complaints. They are serious, aren't they?

What are some of the ways David reminds himself of God's goodness?

Pray for yourself or someone you know who is in a situation too complicated, too crazy, too big for mere humans to sort out. Ask for God's help.

RESPONDING TO HIS WORD

Day 94

REST IN GOD ALONE

My soul finds rest in God alone; my salvation comes from him. —Psalm 62:1

· · · · · · · · · · · · · · · · · · ·

I love rest. I love taking a long walk on a cold winter day, then coming back to my quiet, little home and making a cup of hot tea, grabbing my Bible and a good book, lighting a fire in the fireplace, and just being still. I love Sunday afternoon naps. I love trips to the ocean sitting on a bench and admiring God's amazing handiwork. Yes, rest and I . . . we get along great.

How about you? Seriously, don't most of us love vacation days? Those days are clearly marked "out of the ordinary," and we have no problem letting go and relaxing. Let's face it, though. Luxurious times of stillness and stopping are simply not available every day . . . for any of us. And, during some seasons of life, they are downright hard to find. I wonder how many hours of relaxing by the fire a young mother of triplets has?

At one time, I found myself in a busy season of caregiving. My father-in-law had moved in with us and needed our help with everything: eating, dressing, moving, bathing. I couldn't just leave the house when I felt like it. I was responsible for his needs every day of every week. In order to take a few hours off, I had to find reliable care, and that required preplanning, scheduling—and couldn't happen often.

During that time, I came across this beautiful verse: "My soul finds rest in God alone; my salvation comes from him." How these words challenged and refined me! I asked myself some hard questions. *Does* my soul find rest in God alone? Without the props of fireplaces and ocean views? *Can* I rest in Him in the midst of demanding days and trying times?

I've read stories of Christians in hard places where the wonder-filled kinds of vacation days I love were quite impossible. Corrie Ten Boom in an isolation cell.

Joni Erikson Tada as a teenager, in a bed, paralyzed from the neck down. Yes, there are times we cannot create a "beautiful space" in which to worship God. The question becomes, *Do we know God so well that we can meet with Him anywhere and find rest for our souls in the simple act of being with Him?*

Is it wrong to fight hard to create space to meet with God in our busy lives? No. Sweet Selah Days are a gift to the soul and a means of growing to know God better. Daily quiet times with the luxury of a Bible in our hands on a couch with a cup of tea are a beautiful gift from God. But times like these may not always be available to us. Life can change in a nanosecond.

As long as we can, we should make it a high priority to seek quiet, alone times with God. The purpose of those times is learning to know Him so well that if and when the super hard times ever come, our souls will more easily nestle close to the One we've grown to love. I believe then we will discover that "God Alone" is more than enough, and we will be able to rest in that.

Oh, Father, help me to long for You and find my rest in You in the midst of busy days as well as in the quiet times. Remind me, Lord, that You save me . . . eternally, yes . . . but also daily as I call to You in every need. Remind me to hold on to Your Abba hand all the time . . . when the quiet is easy to find . . . and when it's elusive. God alone. Teach me, Lord. In Your Name, Amen.

. . . .

GOING DEEPER
For those days when you have more time to ponder

Read Psalm 62.

Describe the hard time David was going through.

How did he express through this psalm the comfort he received from God?

Write a prayer of commitment, asking God to help you find rest in "Him alone" right in the midst of your daily living.

RESPONDING TO HIS WORD

Day 95

WHEN CRISIS STRIKES

When Moses' hands grew tired, they took a stone and put it under him and he sat on it. Aaron and Hur held his hands up—one on one side, one on the other—so that his hands remained steady till sunset. —Exodus 17:12

. . . .

Do you ever wish you could schedule your crises? Mine never seem to hit at convenient times. One night, when my girls were in high school, I actually asked if they were planning a crisis later in the evening. If so, I requested they have it early because I was tired. Ha! That did no good, of course. They looked at me like I'd lost my mind. Crises can strike at any time, and when our lives are already full to overflowing, it's terribly hard to find the extra energy to deal with whatever has intruded.

In the verse above, Moses was in crisis. He had been obedient, and God had used him mightily to rescue the Israelites from Egyptian servitude. Now, an enemy was attacking them, and a battle was raging. Moses prayed for victory, and, as long as he lifted his arms to heaven and pleaded with the Lord for help, the Israelites fought valiantly and were winning. But, as the day progressed, the battle continued, and Moses grew weary. As his arms fell, the tide of battle turned. Praying alone for victory was not working. He needed help. The solution was to have Aaron on one side and Hur on the other to hold up Moses' weary hands. Together, they kept his arms steady until the battle was won.

Aren't there times when we are battle weary, crying out for a victory that seems awfully long in coming? We need an "Aaron and a Hur" to hold up *our* weary hands. Who holds you steady when your burden grows too overwhelming? Oh, how I hope you have a few good friends who pray with you and share your heavy load.

Are you in need of prayer warriors to join you in a situation too trying to bear alone? Here are a few suggestions of ways to find an "Aaron and a Hur":

Ask God to reveal who might be the one that could walk with you through the storm.

Invite a godly woman to pray with you and together seek others who are willing to meet regularly to pray about your crisis.

Join a prayer group or Bible study at your church. From that group, ask God to show you one or two women who will share your burden for deeper prayer.

If your troubles are with children, consider joining a Moms in Prayer* group. Some of my deepest friendships began in my Moms in Prayer group. Women who pray in these groups love the Lord dearly and desire to battle for their children and grandchildren through prayer.

Make sure you pray with friends of the same gender. Prayer is a tender, melding time, and praying with someone of the opposite sex can ignite emotions that are not wise.

Father, I thank You for Aaron and Hur and for their example of being there for Moses. Give me helpers like them in my times of need and use me to be an Aaron or Hur for another. Forgive me when I try to go it alone. How I need others, Lord. Guide me to the one who can best lift my arms in times of crisis. In Jesus' Name, Amen.

. . . .

GOING DEEPER
For those days when you have more time to ponder

Read Exodus 17.

This chapter contains two stories about prayer. In each one is a crisis and a need. How are they similar and how are they different?

In the second crisis when Aaron and Hur show up, Joshua is also mentioned. What was his role? Can you think of a situation in your life that involves multiple people serving God in some way?

Do you have two or three trusted friends you can go to for prayer in a crisis? If you do, name them and thank God for them. If you don't, ask God to help you find friends who will hold up your weary hands. Ask God if you are supposed to be that friend to someone else? Enjoy a time of prayer with Him.

*Moms in Prayer International is an organization that brings mothers and grandmothers together once a week to pray for the lives of their children, their grandchildren, and their teachers and schools. For more information, visit MomsInPrayer.org.

• • • • • • • • • • • • • • • •

RESPONDING TO HIS WORD

Day 96

WE DO NOT KNOW WHAT TO DO

Then Jehoshaphat stood up in the assembly of Judah and Jerusalem at the temple of the LORD . . . and said: "LORD, the God of our ancestors, are you not the God who is in heaven? You rule over all the kingdoms of the nations. Power and might are in your hand, and no one can withstand you. . . . But now here are men from Ammon, Moab and Mount Seir. . . . Our God, . . . we have no power to face this vast army that is attacking us. We do not know what to do, but our eyes are on you." —2 Chronicles 20:5-6, 10a, 12

. . . .

Once upon a time, a long time ago, I used to think I knew a lot about running the universe. My prayers were full of advice, giving God suggestions on how to fix a situation very specifically the way I felt would be best. I'd shake my head at others who found themselves in a mess and think how I would have managed it differently. My overconfidence was not pretty.

I used to "manage" my children in my outloud prayers. If our two girls were quarreling, I would stop them and suggest that I pray for them. Somehow, my prayers that they would get along and treat each other with kindness and realize their own selfishness came across as lectures by prayer. Not surprisingly, they didn't much like this, and were not very eager to hear me pray. Now, I understand that.

With age has come awareness of the truth. I am not smart enough to fix things. In fact, the longer I live, the more I identify with Israel's King Jehoshaphat. What did he do when he learned that three armies were on their way to destroy him and God's people? Did he immediately call in his generals to plan a battle? Did he spring into action?

Nope. Instead, with the imminent peril of three armies on the warpath, Jehoshaphat slowed down instead of speeding up. He called an assembly... praised God... and then said the words that are captured forever as one of my favorite Bible prayers: "We do not know what to do, but our eyes are on You."

Oh, Heavenly Father, thank You for this prayer. I don't know how to fix things, Lord. You see the hearts of the people I love. You know their pasts and their futures, their blind spots and their deepest needs. Teach me how to pray for them. Show me the scriptures that will be best for them as I pray. I trust You, Lord, to work in their hearts. Keep my eyes on You, the One who knows all things, loves so deeply, saves so completely. Thank You that You are in charge, and I can leave the managing to You. In Jesus' Name, Amen.

. . . .

GOING DEEPER
For those days when you have more time to ponder

Read 2 Chronicles 20.

Reread 2 Chronicles 20:14-23. Who led the army out to battle?

When you are in a battle, how likely are you to stop, pray, praise . . . before you fight?

Ask God to help you follow Jehoshaphat's example the next time you are experiencing an enemy attack.

. . . .

RESPONDING TO HIS WORD

Day 97

TRIAL TRAINING

In all this you greatly rejoice, though now for a little while you may have had to suffer grief in all kinds of trials. These have come so that the proven genuineness of your faith—of greater worth than gold, which perishes even though refined by fire—may result in praise, glory and honor when Jesus Christ is revealed. —1 Peter 1:6-7

• •

I'm not exactly what you would call an athlete. However, as I grow older, I realize more and more the need to get these muscles moving and lift weights to keep my bones strong. So, I was really enthusiastic when Ray gave me a set of weights on my birthday. "How many pounds are they, Sharon?" asked my then-80-year-old mom. When I told her that I was starting with two-pound weights, she couldn't resist telling me that she works out with five-pound weights. My own mom was way ahead of me. Ah, well. At least I'm moving in the right direction.

After watching a dear friend deal with a shattered shoulder from a simple fall, I realized more than ever the need to strengthen my muscles and bones. From a physician friend and online research, I learned that when a person lifts weights, it causes microscopic tears in the muscle fibers. When these tears heal, the muscles grow bigger and stronger.

When the muscles pull on the bones or when the bones are compressed by weights, the bones actually develop very small cracks in their structure. Within a few days, the body automatically heals these microscopic cracks and that causes an increase in the density of the bones. They grow stronger on the inside because more bone has formed. This assumes, of course, that the exercise is causing enough strain. When you "feel the burn" or experience soreness that's a clue you've actually done some of that useful damage. (Adapted from e-How.com.)

I've learned more about how to protect myself through studying this. It turns out that muscles and bones require stress in order to grow strong—tough enough to withstand a fall. However, this principle of stress causing growth applies to more than my need for exercise. It's a life principle. And that's why we're talking about it.

God uses trials in our lives to create in us strength and resilience and maturity. Hardships and troubles cause "little cracks" in our faith walk and teach us to press in and seek God more forcefully. Pressure and stress force us to rely more deeply on God. When we do, our faith grows, and what seems painful works for our good to make us stronger. Trials are the bodybuilders of our souls. Under pressure, our trust in Him grows and is refined. In fact, God uses our suffering to prove the genuineness of our faith.

It is not fun to walk through trials. It's tough when our faith is tested. Hard to understand, but God has a purpose in it all. May God take every hard road, every tough time in our lives and use it for His great good. Amen?

Father God, it makes sense to me that faith needs to be tested in order to grow stronger. I confess I wish it were not so. Help me, though, to prove genuine in my love for You through trials, so that my faith may result in praise, glory, and honor when Jesus Christ is revealed. In the Name of Jesus, who suffered so much on my behalf, Amen.

. . . .

GOING DEEPER
For those days when you have more time to ponder

Read 1 Peter 1.

Peter packs this chapter with practical words for living. List your favorites.

Rewrite in your own words the value that comes from being refined through trials.

Choose a favorite verse in this chapter. Write it out in full, then thank God for what He is showing you through that verse.

RESPONDING TO HIS WORD

Day 98

WHO'S FIRST?

But I have this against you,
that you have left your first love.
—Revelation 2:4 NASB

• • • • • • • • • • • • • • • • • •

I was thinking about thinking. How do we keep God first in our hearts and our lives and our thoughts? So many others vie for first place honors. I remember a time when God spoke to me about His desire to be first in my thought life.

I was bicycling home from a job as a teenager and daydreaming about a certain Ray Gamble . . . who, it turned out, would someday become my husband. I was pretty much obsessed with him and my mind was on him . . . just about all the time. In fact, I'm pretty certain most nights I fell asleep dreaming about my boyfriend, and most mornings I woke up wondering when I would get to be with him again. Yep, obsessed is the word.

As I biked along that day wondering when Ray would call me next, suddenly God broke into my thinking. He spoke to my heart and asked me to give *Him* my attention. I'm sorry to confess, my first response to this startling request was resentment. Hadn't I met with God that morning? Didn't I lead a Bible study? Didn't I frequently think about Him? Why did He want my thoughts now? I wasn't contemplating bad things. I was just thinking about the guy who made my heart thump faster, who had just made a decision for Christ this past year, the one I hoped to marry someday. What was wrong with that?

Reluctantly, I obeyed. I began talking to God. I asked His blessing on the day ahead. I prayed for my family. I admired the foliage and told God I loved His marvelous creation. Once I began focusing on God, resentment faded away, and I had an amazingly nice little ride.

Interestingly, the next time I was biking, I didn't feel God urging me to turn my thoughts to Him. What was the difference? On the previous ride, I was coming dangerously close to idolizing my boyfriend. God is pretty clear about wanting to be first in our lives, and that includes our thought lives. Placing God firmly on the throne of my heart that day had meant turning my musings from Ray to God.

We must guard against allowing anyone or anything else to dominate our thought lives. Envy begins in our minds. Pride begins in our minds. Worry begins there, and idolatry. Prayer is the best way to fight our wayward thinking. Talking to God through prayer places our attention directly on the King of kings.

When my reflections and focus are centered on the Lord, when I know my mind is under His command, just like that day on the bicycle, His joy and contentment flood my soul. Life is best when God is first. Even in our thoughts . . . especially in our thoughts.

Father, forgive me for the times I allow my mind to walk down forbidden paths. Every time I stray in my thought life, please remind me that I can change what I'm thinking through prayer. Help me turn to You. Help me make it a joyful habit. In Jesus' Name and for His glory, Amen.

GOING DEEPER
For those days when you have more time to ponder

Read Revelation 2.

Focus on the message to Ephesus in verses 1-7. What pleased the Lord about Ephesus? What displeased Him?

Can you think of other Bible verses in which God tells His people He wants to be first? Write them down.

What do you think about the most? Is it your children? Your husband? Your job? Bring it before the Lord and speak to Him about your desire to keep Him first . . . even before _____.

RESPONDING TO HIS WORD

Day 99

BE OF GOOD CHEER

"These things I have spoken to you, that in Me you may have peace. In the world you will have tribulation; but be of good cheer, I have overcome the world." —John 16:33 NKJV

· · · · · · · · · · · · · · · · ·

How thankful I am that Jesus warned us in advance to expect tribulation. Just reading the news these days makes me cry. Literally. Precious, innocent children torn from their families due to senseless wars; earthquakes and famines; sickness and death . . . trouble is everywhere. Add to that, women I personally know who have lost loved ones, others also going through emotional or physical trauma. I just nod my head to this verse and say, "Yes. In this world there is, indeed, much tribulation."

Knowing that Jesus prepared His disciples for tribulation—and He wanted to prepare us—is actually a comfort. Later on, in this same talk, Jesus prays for us all—those living at His time and those of us to come. "I do not pray for these alone, but also for those who will believe in Me through their word" (John 17:20, NKJV). This wonderful discourse with His disciples at the very end of His earthly life—and His prayer—is for *us*. (See John 14-17.)

Here are a few encouragements from Jesus to us in this passage of Scripture:

Our peace is in Him. He spoke these words because He knew how desperately we would need peace. Clearly, we can only find that peace in Him. Oh, how we need to run to Him often and abide in Him so that His peace flows through us in these trying times.

We should not be shocked at hardship and tribulation. It's a sad reality in this fallen world. (As a matter of fact, I actually find myself more shocked—and humbled—by how little tribulation I face. The freedom I have to walk by the ocean,

attend church, and write this book without fear of arrest is amazing. It's a blessing I didn't earn and can't control, but one I treasure.)

Despite all the troubles in the world, Jesus says, "be of good cheer." The reason? He has overcome it all! All this sadness and sickness and terror and cruelty will one day be overturned. He is the ultimate Victor and a time will come when He will dry every tear.

Let's hold on to these truths and be of good cheer as we praise the One who has overcome. Allowing our hearts to be filled with fear and gloom does not serve any good purpose. Remembering that we have a Savior and facing these days with joy in the midst of troubles is liberating. There is a time for sadness, that's true, but Jesus calls us to hang onto cheer in spite of tribulation.

Oh, Father, will You help me to cheer up when I'm depressed about the state of the world? Show me the good in each day and remind me of the ultimate good that is coming when Jesus returns for His bride. Oh, what a glorious day that will be! Thank You for cheering me with Your words. In the Name of Jesus, the Victor, Amen.

. . . .

GOING DEEPER
For those days when you have more time to ponder

Read John 16.

List the ways Jesus comforts His disciples even as He shares hard things with them.

What can you learn from Jesus' words that you can share with others in your life who are experiencing troubled times?

Write three reasons to have good cheer in your life today. Thank God for each of these reasons.

RESPONDING TO HIS WORD

Day 100

BE LIKE A TREE

Blessed is the one
who does not walk in step with the wicked
or stand in the way that sinners take
or sit in the company of mockers,
but whose delight is in the law of the LORD,
and who meditates on his law day and night.
That person is like a tree planted by streams of water,
which yields its fruit in season
and whose leaf does not wither—
whatever they do prospers.
—Psalm 1:1-3

. . . .

Today we come to the end of this devotional book. I hope you have found it to be a journey rich in learning, discovery, and *joy*. We are ending as we began with a look at Psalm 1 and a challenge to "be like a tree" drinking deeply from streams of living water.

Blessed is the one who does not walk in step with the wicked or stand in the way that sinners take or sit in the company of mockers. Let's face it. Practically no one wakes up in the morning and says, "I think I'll go walk with the wicked and

choose sinful ways today while I mock people." Right? And yet, when we plunge right into our days, especially in our culture that has increasingly distanced itself from holiness, we can unintentionally place ourselves in wrong places.

We buy into lies that we must have certain self-care products or we won't be attractive. We watch movies and TV shows that tell us wrong is right, and we start to cheer for the bad guys, who are portrayed as the good guys. We linger over social media much longer than we meant to and wonder why our lives don't look like "theirs." We move at a dizzying pace, trying to "be good" at every single thing we're told we must do, never resting, never stopping, and certainly . . . Never. Ever. Done. We would be far more blessed if we had chosen differently. If you've faithfully read through to this last devotional . . . you have chosen differently.

But whose delight is in the law of the LORD, and who meditates on his law day and night. Delighting in God's laws day and night? How do we reach the point that God's Word is a delight? When His words are so much an internal part of us that day and night—in all sorts of situations—it simply spills out in our words, our actions, our thoughts, because His Word is in us. We have done the deep drinking needed for the living Word to flow through our spiritual veins and arteries.

Discovering that the Word of God is living and active, that the Author of the Bible still speaks through it, is revolutionary. When we grasp that the Bible is a living letter from God to us, reading it ceases to be a dry chore. Instead, it's a treasure trove as we hear from our Beloved. I hope as you have journeyed through these pages with me, this has been your very own personal discovery. God's Word pours life into us. His love and care stream through us as we actively read and believe what He says.

That person is like a tree planted by streams of water, which yields its fruit in season and whose leaf does not wither—whatever they do prospers. When we plant ourselves in His Word, meeting with God daily, we truly grow firm and strong "like a tree." We learn how to live well even in difficult circumstances, with our hands firmly clinging to His. He prunes us, He shapes us, and then He bears fruit through us. Studying God's Word and hearing His own dear voice is delight, indeed.

Heavenly Father, thank You for the gift of Your living Word. Help me to continue this habit of meeting with You each day and hearing You speak. Oh, Lord, how grateful I am for Your love and care for me. Help me to always have a learner's heart. I long for the day when I hear Your voice in Heaven. Until then, help me hear it here on earth. In Jesus' Glorious Name, Amen.

· · · · · · · · · · · · · · · · ·

GOING DEEPER
For those days when you have more time to ponder

Read Psalm 1.

Reflect back on your time in this book. In light of Psalm 1, how have you planted yourself?

List some of the life lessons you've gained as you've studied His Word these past few months.

How do you plan to remain planted "like a tree"? Perhaps you will move to another devotional. Perhaps you'd like to choose a book of the Bible and read it slowly, always being careful to respond to God after you've read. Whatever you decide, write a plan for tomorrow morning, dear one, and *keep going.*

I would love to hear from you. Email me anytime at Sharon@SweetSelah.org. Thank you for taking this journey with me.

· · · · · · · · · · · · · · · · ·

RESPONDING TO HIS WORD

INDEX

MEET THE AUTHOR, SHARON GAMBLE

Hello, Dear Reader!

I wish we could get to know each other over a cup of tea, my favorite way to "meet" someone! Since that's unlikely, here's a bit about me and who I am.

I love people and excitement and parties. Especially tea parties with a few close friends. I also love quiet and creating space to be still with God. In fact, I've grown to love that most of all.

I think nearly all of us know very well without any help how to be busy. But fitting in intentional time to meet with God? That can be tricky. Sharing with women ways to find that time, to know Him more intimately, and grow to love Him more deeply is my passion and my happiness and my sweet spot for sure.

Throughout my life journey, I've collected quotes that have touched me and found Bible verses that have sustained me. I've learned truths that have shaped me. All that God is teaching me in the everyday stories of life, I'm thrilled to pass on to you with a grateful heart.

In fact, God stirred me to form Sweet Selah Ministries that I might share through writing and speaking the insight and thoughts and lessons He is teaching me.

My husband and I live in beautiful New Hampshire with our little "teddy bear pup," Bella Grace. We belong to a great church and love hanging out with our home group every other Friday night.

In the summer, we can often be found bicycling. We have a ton of winding, quaint back roads around here, and our bikes know them all. In the winter, we tromp in the snow and build fires in our fireplace and sip hot chocolate.

We are parents to two wonderful daughters and their dearly-loved husbands, and we are Nina and Papa to an ever-growing bunch of the sweetest grandkids ever.

Along the way, through the ups and downs have come life lessons:

I've failed and learned that failure isn't fatal.
I've overachieved myself into basket-case status.
I've stumbled to God in a mess and felt His arms hold me close.
I've seen the hand of God move in miraculous ways, over and over again.

I'm still on the journey of knowing Him better and loving Him more.

I'd love to stay connected with you. Write me anytime at Sharon@SweetSelah.org and sign up for my blog, *Monday Musings*. You can check it out at SweetSelah.org.

You are loved,
Sharon

CPSIA information can be obtained
at www.ICGtesting.com
Printed in the USA
FSHW021253140621
82369FS

9 781946 369437